Words Their Way®

Words and Strategies for Academic Success

VOLUME I

Savvas Learning Company LLC, 15 East Midland Avenue, Paramus, NJ 07652

ISBN-13: 978-1-4284-3983-2
ISBN-10: 1-4284-3983-8
8 20

SAVVAS
LEARNING COMPANY

Words Their Way

Words and Strategies for Academic Success

Sometimes when I'm reading, I come across words I don't know. That makes it hard to understand what's going on.

Writing is a problem too. My teacher said one way I can improve is to pay attention to the vocabulary in my writing.

Words of Advice

- Learn words. And when you learn them, learn how they work.
- Words have roots; learn to recognize the roots and what they mean.
- Learn vocabulary strategies, such as using context clues and consulting reference materials. These strategies will help you determine the meanings of words.
- Learn the vocabulary of your subject-area classes (Math, Science, Social Studies) and the words that you use in school in general.

Vocabulary is like a tree. It begins with the roots and then just grows and grows.

Contents

Contents

Contents

Contents

LIST 1 phobia

acrophobia
aerophobia
agoraphobia
arachnophobia
claustrophobia
technophobia

Phobia is a Greek root that means "irrational fear."

- Words containing *phobia* have something to do with an abnormal or irrational fear.
- Use *phobia* as a clue to meaning when you come across words that contain this root.

Phobia is a root; *phobia* is also a word with a similar meaning to the root ("irrational fear" of something). When you see words with the root *phobia,* think of *phobia*.

Clues to Meaning Use *phobia* as a clue to the meanings of the underlined words.

Going to a phobia convention could be very interesting! Just think of it—everyone there has some sort of phobia, or fear. Who do you think you might meet?

Look, it's June and Arthur. What a funny pair. You have to wonder how they got together. His agoraphobia makes him extremely fearful of going into public places, while her claustrophobia makes her afraid of being in closed-in spaces.

And over there is Luis, who is afraid of all kinds of insects. You'd think he'd be good friends with Ami, who has arachnophobia, because she is afraid of spiders. But Luis stays away from Ami and hangs around with Jordan, who has technophobia. Jordon breaks out in a cold sweat at the sight of a laptop computer.

Have you met Joaquin and Marie? They have similar fears. His acrophobia makes him afraid of heights, while her aerophobia makes her extremely fearful of flying.

As for me, I didn't go to the phobia convention. How could I! I have what is known as phobophobia—a fear of phobias.

ic

LIST 2

- economic
- futuristic
- genetic
- historic
- organic
- tragic

Ic is a Latin suffix that means "of" or "having to do with."

- When you add *ic* to nouns, they become adjectives.
- To figure out words with the suffix *ic,* identify the base word first and then add the meaning "of" or "having to do with."

When you see *ic,* think of *com**ic*** ("of" or "having to do with" comedy).

Clues to Meaning Use *ic* as a clue to the meanings of the underlined words.

Chris Do you remember the television special we saw about an organic farm where nothing was grown using pesticides? We learned that many people no longer think organic farming is only a futuristic idea, something that will happen years from now. The show made me wonder if most people have the economic means to afford organic foods, which are more expensive.

Sam I've heard that some people have allergies to foods with preservatives. The allergies may be related to their genetic make-up. Researchers think that allergies may be hereditary.

Chris I like television programs about science, but I really like learning about historic events; I watch the History Channel all the time.

Sam Historic movies are usually too tragic for me—you know, stories about the sad things that happen to unfortunate people.

Chris Well, I'd take a tragedy over a horror movie any day. Scary!

In Your Notebook Write each list word and a sentence that uses it. Include context that helps explain the meaning of the word.

Context Clues

One way you can figure out a word's meaning is to look at the text around it, either in the same sentence or in other sentences. What context clues help you figure out what *acrophobia* means?

Andy's seat was in the very top row. As he sat down and looked out at the field far below, his acrophobia kicked in. He felt fear seep over him as his breathing became shallow and his heart began to race.

The first sentence tells you that Andy sat in a high place. The last sentence tells you how he felt about this seat—he felt so much fear that his breathing became shallow and his heart began to race. *Acrophobia* must mean a fear of heights.

Did you know?

The word *organic* has multiple meanings, depending on its use:

- In agriculture, organic food is grown without the use of chemicals.
- In chemistry, organic compounds are those compounds that contain the element carbon.

Apply and Extend

List 1

If you know that *xeno* means "foreign or strange," what does the word *xenophobia* mean? Use *xenophobia* in a sentence that shows you know the meaning of the word.

List 1

Luis has insectophobia, a fear of insects. What do you think *dentophobia* is? *arithmophobia*? What other phobias can you think of?

List 2

The suffix *ic* signals that a word is an adjective. Write two words not on List 2 that have the suffix *ic*. Then define each word. If you want, use a dictionary or go online.

Clue Review Play a word game with one of your classmates. Choose one of the list words. Give your partner a clue about the word. Did your partner guess the word correctly? If not, provide another clue until your partner correctly identifies the word. Then switch roles.

LIST WORDS

ardor
fiery
flustered
passionate
premonition
sensitive
solace
veneration

Use Context as Clues to Meaning

Precise words can help readers understand and picture characters' actions and motivations. When authors use exactly the right words for feelings, their writing comes alive for readers.

Read these sentences.

> Kyle was afraid to speak in public.
> Kyle had **phobic** concerns about speaking in public.

The word ***phobic*** comes from ***phobia*** and means "of or having to do with an irrational fear." Why would an author use *phobic concerns* instead of *afraid* to describe Kyle's feeling?

Read the following debate about banning junk food from school cafeterias. How does the context help you understand the meanings of the underlined words?

- The debate began with Aiden. His strong, spirited feelings came through in his fiery speech in favor of banning junk food in schools. "I believe," he said, "that schools have a major responsibility to combat obesity."
- Quinn, who also had strong emotions about the topic, gave a passionate response. "I think deciding what to eat is the students' responsibility. Schools must be sensitive to students' rights and pay attention to how students feel about those rights."
- With her usual great enthusiasm, Millie spoke up with ardor, hoping to get everyone else excited too. "The Surgeon General has published a report about how many thousands of teens and children are becoming obese every year. Come on, people! Let's get together and fight!"
- Charlie, who seemed flustered and nervous, joined the debate. "I certainly respect what the Surgeon General has to say. I have only veneration for the Surgeon General's report, but who decides what obesity is, and exactly what is junk food?"
- Maya spoke up. "I have a premonition that obesity will only become more of a problem if schools do not ban junk food."
- Charlie countered by saying, "That's not a good reason. A premonition is a vague feeling that something will happen."
- Millie concluded by saying, "Those of us in favor of banning junk food can take solace and be comforted by the fact that schools can offer nutritious food even if junk food is available."

In Your Notebook Write the list words. Next to each word, tell about a time when you had the feeling that the word suggests.

Context Clues

When you read, you can use context, the surrounding words, to determine the meaning of a word. For example, consider the feeling Millie expresses when she speaks up with *ardor*. The context "with her usual enthusiasm" and "hoping to get everyone else excited too" helps you know how Millie felt. Also what she says—"Come on, people! Let's get together and fight!"—helps you know how she sounded when she spoke up with ardor.

You can use a dictionary to check the meaning of the word.

Did you know?

Ardor comes from a Latin word meaning "to burn." If you speak with ardor, you speak with intense feeling, as if you are on fire.

Apply and Extend

- Think about a lively conversation you have heard or participated in. Use list words to describe the feelings that were expressed by each person who spoke.
- Choose one of the list words. Write a sentence or two using context clues to explain the meaning of the word.

Act It Out Put your acting talent to work. Work with several classmates to perform a skit based on the debate in this lesson. Choose a narrator and students to play the characters in the passage. Become your character!

fer

LIST 1

differentiate
fertilizer
inference
reference

Fer is a Greek root that means "bear" or "carry."

- *Fer* can appear at the beginning, middle, or end of a word.

When you see *fer,* think of ***fertile*** (able to "bear" seeds, fruit, or young).

Clues to Meaning Use *fer* as a clue to the meanings of the underlined words.

- That reference book has a lot of facts about reptiles. By knowing this information, what inferences, or conclusions, can you make about lizards?
- The farmer explained that the best way to improve soil was to spread fertilizer on it. However, it was important to know what was different about the fertilizers so you could differentiate between them and choose the best one for you.

port

LIST 2

deport
opportunity
porter
portfolio

Port is a Latin root that means "carry."

- Use *port* as a clue to meaning when you come across words that contain this root.
- The word *portable* has a Latin root and suffix.
  port (carry) + able (capable of) = portable

When you see *port,* think of ***portable*** (able to be "carried").

Clues to Meaning Use *port* as a clue to the meanings of the underlined words.

- Not wanting to miss out on an opportunity to write for his school's literary magazine, Andrew took a thick portfolio of his best writing samples to the advisor's classroom.
- On my family's first train ride to the West Coast, a porter in a blue uniform came to our sleeping car and asked if we needed more pillows.
- To avoid government authorities deporting her back to France, Zoe made sure all of her immigration papers were in order.

LIST 3

transcribe
translate
transmission
transparent

trans

Trans is a Latin prefix that means "across," "over," or "through."

- Words containing *trans* often have to do with moving across or beyond.
- To figure out words with the prefix *trans,* identify the base word first and then add the meaning "across," "over," or "through."

When you see *trans,* think of ***trans****atlantic* (describes going "across" the Atlantic Ocean).

Clues to Meaning Use *trans* as a clue to the meanings of the underlined words.

In 2008, NASA celebrated its fiftieth anniversary by beaming the Beatles' song "Across the Universe" into outer space. The transmission, which was aimed at the star Polaris, should arrive in the year 2439. If extraterrestrials exist, what do you think they will do? Do you think they travel around the universe looking out at the stars through the transparent windows of their spaceship? Do you think they will be able to transcribe the song by writing it down? Will they be able to translate it into their own language?

In Your Notebook Write each list word and its meaning. What context clues helped you figure out word meaning? To check a meaning, use a dictionary.

Context Clues

You can use context clues to figure out a word's meaning. One type of clue is any word or phrase that has a meaning similar to that of the word you want to define. For example, notice how the word *chance* provides a clue to the meaning of the list word *opportunity* in the sentence below.

When Gilberto had the opportunity to make a 3-pointer in the basketball game, he decided to take the chance and shot the ball a long distance, making the basket.

When trying to figure out an unfamiliar word, look for a word or phrase that might have a similar meaning. Consult a dictionary to check the meaning.

Apply and Extend

List 1

The word *reference* has several meanings and can be used as both an adjective and a noun. Write two sentences that show different meanings of *reference* when it is used as a noun. You may want to use a dictionary to check meanings.

List 2

Write a question about one of the words that contains *port*, showing that you understand the meaning of the word. An example question for the word *portfolio* might be the following: *Which word can mean both a carrying case and the set of documents or drawings carried in such a case?*

List 3

Choose a list word and write a sentence for it, but do not write in the word. Be sure to include context as clues to the word's meaning. Switch sentences with a partner and supply each other's words.

Did you know?

The base word of *inference* is *infer*, which means "to find out what something means," or "to conclude." *Imply* means "to express indirectly," or "to suggest." If you *infer* what someone *implies*, then you understand what he or she means.

Rap It Up Work with a classmate. Using a list word and its meaning, create a short poem or rap like this one. Compile your rap or poem with those of classmates into a Rap It Up notebook.

Opportunity

When opportunity knocks,
Like a chance in a box,
Be open. Be aware,
And let yourself take the dare.

LIST WORDS

association
denotation
dialect
etymology
fantasy
nuance
syllabication
usage

Use Context as Clues to Meaning

You read many things every day, some better written than others. What makes a story interesting? What is it about an article that keeps you engaged? It's all in the way it's written. In other words, it's the words. The list words in this lesson are ones you can use to communicate about what you write. You may come across them in your language arts class.

Read about writing creatively. How does the context help you understand the meanings of the underlined words?

When you sit down to write a story, what do you think about? Do you prefer to write about real places and people? Or do you think of imaginary places and characters that would fit in a fantasy? Perhaps you have your own ways to help you get ready to write. One way is to start with word association to set your scene. For example, what does the word *moonlight* make you think of? What could happen in a land of ice and snow? You might invent dialects (perhaps a version of Elvish?) for your characters to speak. Or you might describe the nuances of how characters dress or other little differences in the way they look. However, even your most creative writing should be grounded in the proper usage of English grammar; knowing how to use parts of speech correctly is necessary for good writing. Also, if you want to use a word but are unsure of its denotation, or exact meaning, try looking it up in a dictionary. Besides the meaning, a dictionary entry may include an etymology, or word history. A dictionary is also a good source for learning about syllabication, the process of dividing words into syllables. So gather your creative thoughts and write away!

In Your Notebook Write your own paragraph about creative writing, using the list words. To check a meaning, use a dictionary.

Using a Dictionary

A dictionary is an invaluable reference source. Whenever you want to learn about words, start with a dictionary. It contains thousands of words, which are listed in alphabetical order. Each word has an entry that provides information about the word: spelling, pronunciation, definition, use, history. A dictionary can be a printed book or online.

Consult a dictionary when you want to

- find the pronunciation of a word
- verify a word's meaning
- determine a word's precise meaning
- clarify a word's part of speech
- learn about a word's etymology

Did you know?

Nuance comes from the Latin, *nubes,* for clouds. Some experts believe the subtle shadings of clouds contributed to the word's modern meaning.

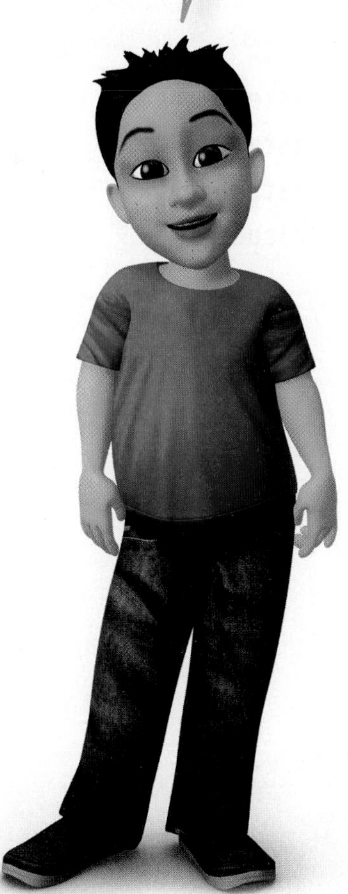

Apply and Extend

- *Dialect,* from the Greek for "talk," means a regional variation in language. In some parts of the United States, carbonated drinks are called sodas. Elsewhere they are known as pop or tonic. With a partner, come up with a list of words that are common in your regional dialect. You can check online for resources on regional English.

- Write a riddle using list words. For example: *If I used the exact definition of a word, did I use a nuance or a denotation?* Exchange riddles with a partner and answer each other's riddles.

Word History Choose an interesting word from this week's lesson. What can you find out about the history and origins of your word? Try to answer these questions:

- From which language did your word derive?
- What is its first recorded instance of use in the English language?
- What is one interesting fact you learned about the word?
- List related words that you find.

LESSON 5 Word Parts and Meanings

stel, astr, aster, ist

LIST 1

interstellar
stellar

stel

Stel is a Latin root that means "star."

- Words containing *stel* usually have something to do with the stars.
- Use *stel* as a clue to meaning when you come across words that contain this root.

When you see *stel,* think of *con**stel**lation* (a group of "stars").

Clues to Meaning Use *stel* as a clue to the meanings of the underlined words.

- Interstellar space flight would allow us to travel between the stars from our solar system to another one that is light-years away.
- After her stellar performance with the Metropolitan Symphony, many people considered Irma to be a star violinist.

LIST 2

aster
asterisk
astronomy
disaster

astr, aster

Astr is a Greek root that means "star." Another way to spell this root is ***aster***.

- Words containing *astr* or *aster* usually have something to do with the stars.

When you see *astr* or *aster,* think of ***astronaut*** (a person who travels among the "stars").

Clues to Meaning Use *astr* and *aster* as clues to the meanings of the underlined words.

Astrid wondered to herself, "What an odd assortment of words! How do they relate to *astr* or *aster,* meaning 'star'?" She realized, "Astronomy is the scientific study of stars. That's clear enough. I know an asterisk is a punctuation mark that looks a bit like a star. What is an aster?" With some research, she found pictures of asters, flowers whose starburst-like petals gave them their name. Then Astrid was stumped. "I know a disaster is a terrible event that causes suffering and loss. How does that relate to stars? I'll have to investigate further."

ist

LIST 3

anthropologist
dentist
egotist
illusionist
medalist
realist

The Greek suffix *ist* means "one who believes, does, or is an expert in something."

- Words ending with the suffix *ist* refer to people who believe or do something or are specialists in their field.
- Use *ist* as a clue to meaning when you come across words that contain this suffix.

ANCHOR WORD scient**ist**

When you see *ist,* think of *scient**ist*** (a person who is an "expert" in science).

Clues to Meaning Use *ist* as a clue to the meanings of the underlined words.

- The anthropologist had just finished her study of peoples who live in the Andes Mountains.
- I brush my teeth twice a day, so I am never afraid to have the dentist check my teeth.
- I do not like to work on projects with people who are egotists. They just talk and talk about themselves too much.
- Juan is a talented illusionist. He made the audience at his magic show think that he disappeared.
- Sarah wants to be the best in swimming races and win medals. Someday, she hopes to be an Olympic medalist.
- Matt would love to get a new camera, but he is a realist. He knows that he can't afford the camera he wants.

In Your Notebook Use each list word in a sentence that contains a context clue to the word's meaning. To check a meaning, use a dictionary.

Using a Glossary

A glossary is a specialized dictionary that covers a set of related words. The words might all have to do with a particular topic or area of knowledge. Textbooks often have glossaries at the back where words taught throughout the book are gathered in one place for easy reference. While a dictionary might give you any number of definitions for a word, a glossary may offer the one or two definitions you need for what you are reading. The glossary at the back of this book covers the words presented in the lessons. You may want to consult it first when looking up your list words.

Did you know?

Disaster has the same root as *astrology*, which is the study of the stars to predict the future. In ancient times, some people believed that bad luck resulted from a bad arrangement of the stars.

Apply and Extend

List 1

Write a question about one of the words that contains *stel*, showing that you understand the meaning of the word. An example question for the word *interstellar* is: *Which word describes something between the stars?*

List 2

Write one sentence using as many of the list words as you can. Challenge yourself. Can you use all four words in one sentence?

List 3

Write a riddle for one of the list words. An example riddle for the word *dentist* is: *Which word names someone who would be really interested in your teeth?*

Graphic Gallery Use your skills as a cartoonist to create a comic strip using words from this week's lesson. Draw pictures and write dialogue or use an online program to create the graphic text. How many of the words can you use? Compile the class's comic strips into a Graphic Gallery.

LIST WORDS

asteroid
astronomer
black hole
experimental
galaxy
mechanics
meteor
meteorite

Use Context as Clues to Meaning

When you study astronomy, you learn about the sun, moon, planets, and stars. In the word *astronomy, astro* comes from the Greek root *astr,* which means "star." *Nom* comes from the Greek root *nomia,* which refers to a law or an arrangement. Astronomy is the study of the natural laws that govern the stars. To the right are more words related to the study of the stars and space. You may come across these words in your science class.

The words *astronomy* and *astronomer* are related. *Astronomer* ends with the suffix *er,* which comes from the Latin suffix *arius,* meaning "one who engages in an activity."

Read the dialogue below. How does the context help you understand the meanings of the underlined words?

Captain I just saw a meteor flash by.

Tork Unlikely, Captain, as we are in deep space and there is no atmosphere to heat up a moving object and make it speed past us. I'm sure you know it's not an asteroid either, one of those small, rocky bodies that orbit the sun looking like a small star.

Captain I don't need a lecture on elementary astronomy or the effects of forces. I know all about the mechanics of atmospheric friction, Tork. Let's just focus on not getting sucked into that huge black hole. If we get sucked in, we won't be able to escape!

Tork Also, technically, the moving object would be called a meteoroid because it has not yet entered Earth's atmosphere.

Captain [muttering] I knew it was a bad idea to choose an astronomer to be my first officer. [to Tork] I knew that, of course. I found a meteoroid once in my backyard.

Tork Technically, if you found it in your backyard, it was a meteorite, because it had reached Earth without burning up.

Captain [muttering] Two hundred billion stars in the galaxy, and I have to be flying around the same one as this clown. [to Tork] Let's conduct an experimental investigation to find out how long a first officer can survive in a vacuum.

In Your Notebook Write each list word and its meaning. Then write the words or phrases from the dialogue that helped you figure out the meaning of each word.

Word Story

The English name of our galaxias—the Milky Way—is a translation of the Latin phrase *Via Lactea.* The word *galaxy* itself comes from the Greek word *galaxias,* which means "milky." When you look lengthwise through the plane of the galaxy, you see many more stars than you do when you look above or below it. The concentrated area appears in the night sky as a pale stripe, which the ancient Romans thought of as a "milky" way or road.

Did you know?

A *black hole* is the material left over from a collapsed star that has become so dense that even its atomic structure collapses. No light can escape it.

Apply and Extend

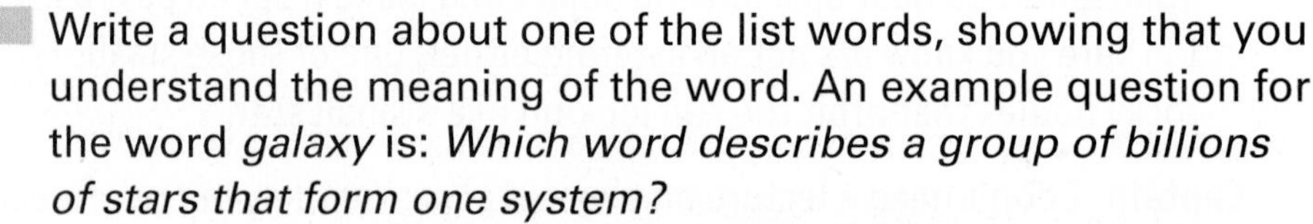

- Write a question about one of the list words, showing that you understand the meaning of the word. An example question for the word *galaxy* is: *Which word describes a group of billions of stars that form one system?*

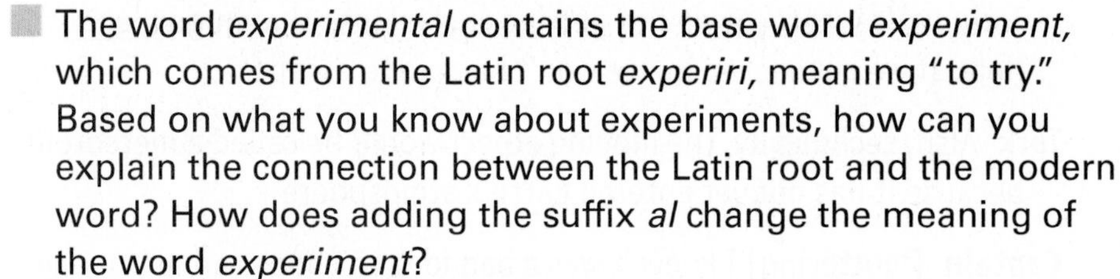

- The word *experimental* contains the base word *experiment,* which comes from the Latin root *experiri,* meaning "to try." Based on what you know about experiments, how can you explain the connection between the Latin root and the modern word? How does adding the suffix *al* change the meaning of the word *experiment*?

Act It Out Put your writing and acting talent to work. Work with a classmate to continue the dialogue between the Captain and Tork. Then perform a skit involving these brave astronauts!

dict

LIST 1

contradict
dictate
dictator
verdict

Dict is a Latin root that means "say" or "speak."

- Words containing *dict* usually have something to do with saying or speaking words.
- Use *dict* as a clue to meaning when you come across words that contain this root.

When you see *dict,* think of ***predict*** ("say" what will happen before it does).

Clues to Meaning Use *dict* as a clue to the meanings of the underlined words.

- Because the dictator had complete control of the government, people were afraid to speak out against him or contradict what he said.
- In a clear voice, the judge dictated what the jury had decided, and the court reporter recorded the verdict.

graph

LIST 2

biography
cartography
graphic
telegraph

Graph is a Greek root that means "to write."

- The word *autograph* has two Greek roots.

auto (self) + graph (to write) = autograph

When you see *graph,* think of *auto**graph*** (someone, who is usually famous, "writes" his or her name for someone else).

Clues to Meaning Use *graph* as a clue to the meanings of the underlined words.

Pat Do you have any books about Samuel Morse's life? He had a lot to do with the telegraph. How cool that he put together a device that used a code of dots and dashes to send messages.

Librarian Many authors have written about Samuel Morse's life. Here's one biography that you might like. This book has wonderful graphic descriptions. The words really help you see Morse and his telegraph.

Pat Or maybe I should read about cartography. I'm very interested in mapmaking too. Hmmm. Telegraphs or maps, that is the question!

LIST 3

co

coauthor
coeducational
coexist
coworker

Co is a Latin prefix that means "with" or "together."

- To figure out words with the prefix *co,* identify the base word first and then add the meaning "with" or "together."

When you see *co,* think of ***copilot*** (person who works "together with" the main pilot to fly an aircraft and is second in command).

Clues to Meaning Use *co* as a clue to the meanings of the underlined words.

Have you and your friends ever thought about forming a band? What kind of music would you play, other people's or your own? If you wrote your own songs and you were one of the coauthors, would you write the words or the tune? Remember, the words and melody need to coexist, working together each note of the way. That means that you and your coworkers need to work together for the good of the song. You can use the rules you follow to get along with the boys and girls in your coeducational classes as a model. Are you ready to tune up?

In Your Notebook Write each list word and its meaning. What context clues helped you figure out word meaning? To check a meaning, use a dictionary.

Synonym Study

Contradict has the Greek root *contra,* which means "against," and the Latin root *dict.* To contradict something is to "speak against" it by saying it is not true. If you contradict someone, you say the opposite of what that person has said. *Contradict* has several synonyms; a synonym is a word that means the same or nearly the same as another word. Some synonyms for *contradict* are *deny, disagree, oppose, dispute, challenge.*

How do you know which synonyms to use in your writing? Use the word that most precisely expresses what you want to say. You can check a thesaurus or dictionary to confirm meanings.

Apply and Extend

List 1

Write a question about one of the words that contains *dict,* showing that you understand the meaning of the word. An example question for the word *verdict* is: *Which word is something that is said at the end of a trial?*

List 2

Write one sentence using as many of the list words as you can. Challenge yourself. Can you use all four words in one sentence?

List 3

Think about how *coauthor, coworker,* and *colleague* are related in meaning. Is a coworker a colleague? Can a coauthor be a colleague? Write a sentence or two, using these three words.

Word Part Invention How much of a wordsmith are you? With a partner, combine word parts from this lesson with other letters or syllables to invent a new word. Then write a definition for the word based on the meanings of the word parts. Share the word and definition with classmates.

Did you know?

The prefix *col,* like *co,* means "with" or "together." When you see a word that begins with *col,* such as *colleague,* you can figure out its meaning—someone who works together with someone else.

LIST WORDS

competition
consumer
efficiency
monopoly
mortgage
stockholder
volatility
yield

Use Context as Clues to Meaning

The prefix *co* means "with" or "together." A competition is a contest "with" someone, such as a swimming competition. In business, merchants are in competition "with" each other to win customers to buy their goods and services. At the left are more words related to competition, goods, and services. You may come across these words in your social studies class.

Read about economics, the study of producing, distributing, and consuming goods and services. How does the context help you understand the meanings of the underlined words?

An economy is based on producers who provide goods and services and consumers who buy their goods and services.

You are a consumer if you buy goods and services for personal use. A consumer who buys property usually takes out a mortgage, which is a loan that gives the bank a legal right or claim to the property if the consumer does not make payments on the loan.

If you have a smart phone, you may prefer a particular brand. Many companies produce smart phones and are in competition with each other to attract you and other customers to their products. Not wasting time and money leads to efficiency, which is needed to create products people will want. What if a majority of smart phone owners start buying one brand? Then the company receives the largest share of business, controls the market, and becomes a monopoly.

Suppose you think the company that makes your favorite smart phone is going to be successful and make money. You have been saving your allowance and want to invest to make it grow. You decide to buy a share of stock in the company. That means you become a stockholder in the company and own a small part of it. You want to earn the highest possible yield, or return on your investment. Each stock's value can have volatility, or rapid changes, because the worth of the company issuing the stock can go up or down suddenly.

In Your Notebook Write each list word and its meaning. To check a meaning, use a dictionary.

Antonym Study

Notice how the word *volatility* is used in these sentences.

Mila's volatility shows her changeable, moody nature.

Once the owner started paying regular attention to the cat, the cat's volatility changed to calmness.

In the first sentence, *volatility* is defined by the context "changeable" and "moody." In the second sentence, an antonym helps you figure out the meaning of *volatility.* An antonym is a word that means the opposite of another word. *Calmness* is the antonym, or opposite, of *volatility.*

One way you can find antonyms is to search online. You can verify meanings by consulting a thesaurus or dictionary.

Did you know?

Efficiency can refer to the ratio of work performed to the energy supplied, a very small apartment, or any action done without waste.

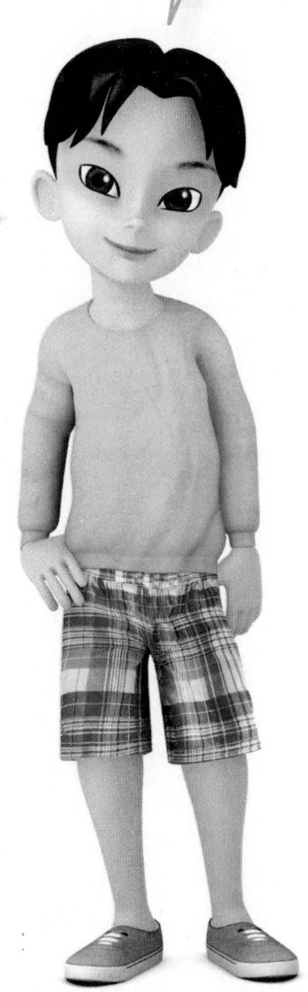

Apply and Extend

- *Monopoly* comes from the combining form *mono,* which means "having one; single" and the Greek word for "to sell." Explain how the word parts help you define the word *monopoly.* Challenge yourself to think of an example of a monopoly.
- Choose one of the list words and write other words you might study in connection with that list word in an economics lesson. For *stockholder,* you might list *market, banks, interest rates, stocks,* and *bonds.*

Graphic Gallery Use your skills as a cartoonist to create a comic strip using words from this week's lesson. Draw pictures and write dialogue or use an online program to create the graphic text. How many of the words can you use? Work together with classmates to compile the class's comic strips into a Graphic Gallery.

LIST 1 pos, pon

component
disposable
exponent
expose
exposition
postpone
proponent
proposition

Pos is a Latin root that means "put" or "place." Another way to spell this root is ***pon***.

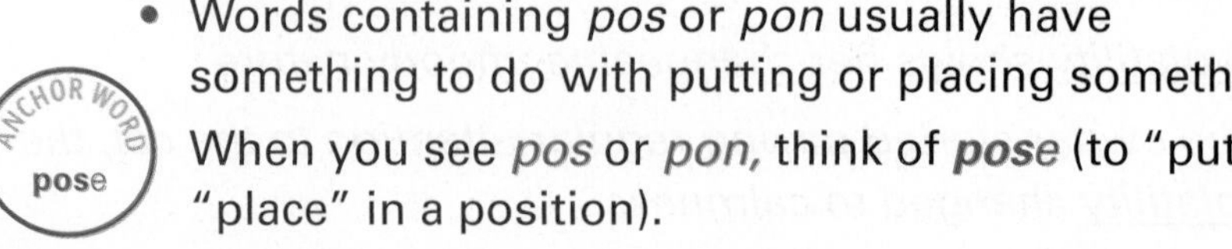

- Words containing *pos* or *pon* usually have something to do with putting or placing something.

When you see *pos* or *pon,* think of ***pose*** (to "put" or "place" in a position).

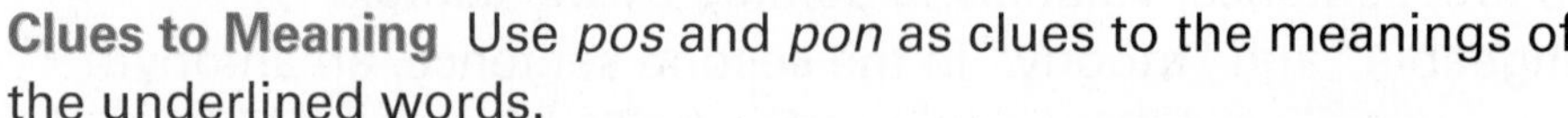

Clues to Meaning Use *pos* and *pon* as clues to the meanings of the underlined words.

Avery's mom is an example for her neighbors because she recycles everything that can be recycled and is a strong exponent of the recycling center. At meetings she gives expositions, talks that explain why recycling is necessary. Avery, who is running for class president, is following her mother's lead. In her campaign Avery is proposing that people stop using disposable plastic bags. Even though they are designed to be thrown away, she thinks that people unthinkingly throw them away rather than recycle them. "Some components that go into making plastics are harmful," she argues. "We need to make up our minds now to stop using plastics. If we keep postponing this decision, we will regret it."

Max is Avery's rival in the election for class president. He also wants to save the environment and is a proponent of recycling. Yet he doesn't believe that plastic products can be eliminated completely. His proposal is to encourage recycling by placing more bins in the downtown area. This proposition is the focus of his campaign. He claims he will reveal facts to expose problems in Avery's proposals, making known why they won't work.

com, con

LIST 2

commemorate
commerce
conclusion
congenial

Com is a Latin prefix that means "together" or "with." Another way to spell this prefix is ***con***.

- The word *companion* has two Latin roots.

com (with) + pani (bread) = companion

When you see *com* or *con,* think of ***com****panion* (a person who spends time, or breaks bread, "with" another).

Clues to Meaning Use *com* and *con* as clues to the meanings of the underlined words.

- Everyone on Dara's team got along well so it was no problem for this congenial team to decide who would research what. Dara's research uncovered an interesting piece of history to contribute to her team's report. During World War I, Germany attacked Great Britain's merchant ships to disrupt the commerce, or buying and selling of goods, between nations and the transportation of supplies.
- A group of recent veterans who wanted to remember the end of World War I gathered to commemorate its conclusion. They honored the memory of soldiers who served in that war.

In Your Notebook Write the list words and their meanings. To check a meaning, use a dictionary.

Using a Thesaurus

If you need a synonym or an antonym for a word, such as *congenial*, you can use a thesaurus; to locate a particular word, you would look in the index at the back of the book to find the page number or numbers on which the word is described. Other thesauruses are organized alphabetically. In a thesaurus entry, you can expect to find information such as the word's part of speech, synonyms, and antonyms. Using a thesaurus can help you find precise, descriptive words to improve your writing.

Apply and Extend

List 1

Consider the meaning of *pos* or *pon* and explain how it relates to the meaning of one of the list words. For example, *disposable* could be defined as "able to be *put* away or *placed* in the garbage after using." Choose two different words and connect their meanings to the meaning of *pos* or *pon*. You may want to use a dictionary.

List 1

Think about how *exponent, expose,* and *exposition* are related in meaning. Can an exponent expose a problem? Can an exponent produce exposition? Write one or two sentences using these three words.

List 2

Write a question about one of the words that contains the prefix *com* or *con* to show that you understand the meaning of the word. An example question for the word *congenial* might be: *Which word describes a friendly, agreeable person?*

Word History Choose an interesting word from this lesson. What can you find out about the history and origins of your word?

- From which language did your word derive?
- What is the first recorded instance of its use in the English language?
- What is one interesting fact you learned about the word?

LIST WORDS

absolute value
additive
complex fraction
compound interest
opposite
order of operations
rational number
simple interest

Use Context as Clues to Meaning

The word *opposite* comes from the Latin *opponere,* which means "set against." *Opposite* means "place against or in a different direction." In mathematics, two numbers are *opposite* if they are the same distance from 0 and on opposite sides of a number line, for example –3 and +3.

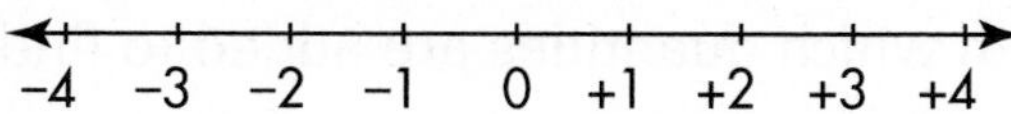

At the right are more words related to math. You may come across these words in your math class.

Read the following sentences. How does the context help you understand the meanings of the underlined words?

- The absolute value of a number is the positive value of a number regardless of its + or – sign. The number is written between two vertical, parallel lines, and identifies the number's distance from zero.
- The word additive is an adjective used to describe numbers that are added together, or combined, in addition.
- The order of operations is the sequence you follow to solve a math problem. First, complete the work in parentheses; then, simplify exponents (e.g, 5^2, or five squared); then, multiply and divide from left to right; and finally, add and subtract from left to right.
- In math, opposite numbers have opposite signs (+ and –). If you add two opposite numbers, for example + 4 and –4, the answer is 0.
- A fraction is part of a whole number (for example, $\frac{1}{2}$ or $\frac{2}{3}$). In a complex fraction, the numerator or denominator or both contain a fraction. (for example, $\frac{\frac{1}{2}}{\frac{3}{4}}$)
- A rational number is a number that can be written as a ratio and named as a fraction or a decimal.
- When you deposit money in a savings account, the bank often will pay you to leave your money there. The money that the bank pays you is called *interest.* Simple interest is money you earn only on the original amount you deposited. Compound interest is money earned on the amount deposited plus the interest that is added periodically.

In Your Notebook Write each term in your notebook. Next to each term, write an example showing your understanding of the term.

Multiple Meanings

Some words have different meanings, depending on how they are used. For example, in mathematics, *additive* refers to a function, or operation, in which quantities are added to find the sum. *Additive* also refers to something that is added to change or improve the quality of a product. For example, a food additive is a substance added directly to food during processing. It may be added to preserve the food or give it color.

Did you know?

Ideas often come in pairs of opposites, such as big/little, before/after, for/against. Prefixes also come in pairs of opposites, such as *macro/micro, mega/mini, pro/anti, over/under, pre/post,* and *sub/super.*

Apply and Extend

- The word *opposite* has more than one meaning. In this lesson, you learned the meaning of *opposite* when used in mathematics. However, *opposite* also has a general meaning that you are probably more familiar with. Use *opposite* in a sentence that shows its mathematical meaning and in a sentence that shows its general meaning.

- Choose one of the list words and write an example to illustrate the meaning. To show your understanding of *simple interest,* you could write an equation: $100 (deposit) x .03 (interest) = $3.00.

Clue Review Play a word game with a partner. Choose one of the list words. Give your partner a clue about the word. Did your partner guess the word correctly? If not, provide another clue until your partner correctly identifies the word. Then switch roles.

vert, vers

LIST 1

adversary
conversion
diversion
divert
inverse
revert
versatile
vertical

Vert is a Latin root that means "turn." Another way to spell this root is ***vers***.

- Words containing *vert* or *vers* usually have something to do with turning.

ANCHOR WORD convert

When you see *vert* or *vers,* think of *con**vert*** ("turning" to something else).

Clues to Meaning Use *vert* or *vers* as clues to the meanings of the underlined words.

She had to admit, her adversary was versatile. "That guy I'm playing against can do a million things well, including playing chess!" Since her conversion to chess from checkers was much too recent to make her a worthy opponent, her only hope was to create a diversion to distract him. "What's that over there?" she cried suddenly, pointing to the tall, vertical window across the room. Unfortunately, her scheme had an inverse effect, as her opponent hunkered down and concentrated even harder. She sensed it was time to revert to her original plan, which was to defend her king with all the pieces that she had left. If only she hadn't chosen chess to divert herself while her checkers partner was out of town!

de

LIST 2

dehydrate
demolish

De is a Latin prefix that means "remove" or "opposite."

- The word *deforest* has the Latin prefix *de* and the base word *forest.* To figure out its meaning, identify the root or base word first and then add the meaning "remove" or "opposite."

  de (remove) + forest = deforest

When you see *de,* think of ***de**forest* (to "remove" a forest).

Clues to Meaning Use *de* as a clue to the meanings of the underlined words.

- One way to preserve fruits and vegetables is to dehydrate them using enough heat to draw out the moisture.
- Wrecking balls are often used to demolish buildings.

LIST 3 re

reclaim
renew

Re is a Latin prefix that means "again."

- To figure out words with the prefix *re*, identify the base word first and then add the meaning "again."

When you see *re,* think of *recapture* (to seize "again").

Clues to Meaning Use *re* as a clue to the meanings of the underlined words.

Jesse I plan to reclaim the title of Guitar King in this year's Battle of the Bands. It was embarrassing to lose the title last year.

Josiah Well, then, you'd better renew your efforts and practice more. Jason plays a mean riff and will be tough to beat.

In Your Notebook Write each list word in a sentence that contains at least one context clue to the word's meaning. To check a meaning, use a dictionary.

Biblical Allusions

Every day we revert—we go back to original plans, ways of doing things, old beliefs, conversations, and stories. When you make a biblical allusion, you are reverting to an original Bible story for a reference. For example, calling someone who helps others a "Good Samaritan" is a reference to the biblical story of a man who helped a wounded man. If you call someone "Goliath," chances are the person is large or powerful. Goliath was a giant warrior in the Bible, who stood more than nine feet tall.

Biblical allusions are used all the time. You see, read, and hear them in movies, plays, literature, news articles, and speeches. You probably even use them in your own conversations and writing.

Apply and Extend

List 1

Describe in one or two sentences the relationship between the words *divert* and *diversion*. What parts of speech are they? Use them in a sentence.

List 2

Think about what it means to be dehydrated. Write one or two sentences showing that you understand the meaning of the word.

List 3

Think about the prefix *re*, which means "again." Write a sentence or two that uses the list words *reclaim* and *renew* and one other word that starts with *re*.

Have you heard this expression?

Vice versa, which means "the other way around," contains two Latin roots meaning "turn": *vicis* and *vers*. This expression indicates that the order of two things or people is reversed, or "turned."

Word Part Invention How much of a wordsmith are you? With a partner, combine word parts from this lesson with other letters or syllables to invent a new word. Then write a definition for the word based on the meanings of the word parts. Share the word and definition with classmates.

LIST WORDS

amble
bolt
frantically
hasten
nonchalantly
saunter
scurry
trudge

Use Context as Clues to Meaning

The word *demolish* includes the Latin prefix *de,* which means "opposite," and the Latin word *moliri,* which means "build."

de (opposite) + moliri (build) = demolish (to destroy)

Action words like *demolish* help create a vivid image in a reader's mind. Picture this sentence as you read it: *When the deer found itself trapped in the yard, it demolished the fence to escape.*

In addition to *demolish,* English has many other words to describe movement—words that communicate precise kinds of actions. Good writers use a variety of precise words to paint exciting pictures for their readers. Writers can add words, such as adverbs, to help describe movement even more precisely.

For example, the adverb *frantically* comes from the same Greek root as *frantic,* which means "wild with rage, fear, or another emotion." Read the sentence with the word *frantically* added: *When the deer found itself trapped in the yard, it frantically demolished the fence to escape.* How does this adverb change how you picture the deer's movement?

Read the following paragraph. How does the context help you understand the meanings of the underlined words?

Jackson awoke and sat straight up. He remembered what day it was, and he didn't want to be late. He bolted out of bed, his feet thumping the floor as he swiftly jumped down. He threw on his clothes and hastened downstairs for a quick breakfast. He then searched frantically for his homework, looking everywhere and feeling terrified that it might be lost. Suddenly, he saw it on the table. He stuffed it in his backpack and ran out the door. "This is no day to saunter—I cannot take my time," he told himself, as he sprinted down the street. Squirrels scurried out of his way and up nearby trees. Neighborhood kids, still half-asleep, trudged slowly toward school. As he approached the building, he calmed down, ambled casually up the steps, and pushed nonchalantly on the door, trying not to appear eager. Locked! He'd have to wait until 8 a.m. to see if he'd made the cut for the baseball team.

In Your Notebook Write the list words. Next to each word, describe the picture it creates for you.

Word Story

Amble comes from a Latin word meaning "walk." For a long time, the word was only applied to horses or riders on horseback. In English today, *amble* means "walk slowly." *Amble* appears as a base word in *funambulist* ("tightrope walker"), *somnambulist* ("sleepwalker"), and *ambulatory* ("capable of walking").

Did you know?

Bolt once named a type of crossbow arrow, and the word's meaning, "run away," comes from the flight of that arrow. *Bolt of lightning* also comes from this origin.

Apply and Extend

- Think about a sporting event or movie you have seen recently. Write two or three sentences using list words to describe how the players or actors moved at any point in the action.
- Select one list word and identify both an antonym (opposite meaning) and a synonym (similar meaning) for it. The antonym and synonym can be list words or different words. Write a sentence or two using all three words. Include context that shows you understand the meaning of each word.

Word History Choose an interesting movement word from this week's lesson. What can you find out about the history and origins of your word? Answer the following questions:

- From what language did your word derive?
- What is the first recorded instance of its use in the English language?
- What is one interesting fact you learned about the word?
- List related words that you find.

LIST 1 scrib, script

description
indescribable
inscribe
manuscript
prescribe
scripture
subscribe
subscription

Scrib is a Latin root that means "write." Another way to spell this root is ***script***.

- Words containing *scrib* or *script* usually have something to do with writing.

When you see *scrib* or *script,* think of ***scrib**ble* ("write" carelessly or hastily).

Clues to Meaning Use *scrib* and *script* as clues to the meanings of the underlined words.

- The police were able to identify the burglar from the witness's description of what the thief looked like.
- Sharona thought that the concert was indescribable. She tried, but she could not find words that were as beautiful as the music.
- People sometimes put up a statue in honor of a famous person and inscribe the person's name at the bottom.
- After Jackson's doctor prescribed him an inhaler to help control his asthma, he took the doctor's written order to the pharmacy.
- After completing her manuscript, J. K. Rowling sent it off to the publisher to be made into a Harry Potter book.
- Many religions have a sacred scripture, such as the Bible or Koran, in which important stories and teachings are recorded.
- To subscribe to that magazine, you need to fill out this form and send the publisher twelve dollars for a one-year subscription. In fact, I need to renew my subscription so that I keep getting the magazine every month.

gram

LIST 2

anagram
grammar
programmer
telegram

Gram is a Greek root that means "thing written."

- Words containing *gram* usually have to do with something that is written.
- Use *gram* as a clue to meaning when you come across words that contain this root.

When you see *gram,* think of *diagram* (a drawing that shows how something is constructed or is "written" in pictures).

Clues to Meaning Use *gram* as a clue to the meanings of the underlined words.

- The anagrams for Andrew's name are *warned* and *wander;* those words are written using the same letters as the letters in his name.
- It is important to understand the rules of English grammar in order to write and speak correctly.
- The programmer bought a new, faster computer so that he could write software more quickly.
- People used to get telegrams with bad news; these telegraphed messages written onto slips of paper are rarely sent anymore.

In Your Notebook Write each list word and its meaning. What context clues helped you figure out word meaning? To check a meaning, use a dictionary.

Figurative Language

Often, writers use words in ways that are outside the exact meanings of those words but add beauty to their writing. For example, the literal, or dictionary, meaning of the word *inscribe* is "write or engrave words on stone, paper, or metal." A writer might use the word in a more figurative way, saying, perhaps, "you have inscribed your name on my heart." See how figurative language makes the literature you read more interesting and beautiful.

LESSON 13

Apply and Extend

Did you know?

Some words have prefixes that look alike but don't mean the same thing. For example, the prefix *in* means "not" in the word *indescribable* and "in" or "onto" in the word *inscribe*.

List 1

The words *description* and *subscription* have the base words *describe* and *subscribe*, which are verbs. How does adding the suffix *tion* change the part of speech of these base words? Write a sentence for each word, showing you understand the words' meanings.

List 1

The word *scribe,* which shares the same root as *inscribe* and *manuscript*, means "a person who copies manuscripts." Write a sentence or two using these three words. Use context that shows you understand the meanings of the words.

List 2

Work with a partner to create anagrams of some of the students' names in your class. Share your favorite anagram with the class.

Rap It Up Working with a classmate, choose a word from this lesson. Use the word and its definition to create a short poem or rap. Compile your rap with other classmates' raps into a Rap It Up notebook. Here is an example.

Telegram

I'm sending you a telegram
to let you know just how I am
and how I feel about you, ma'am.
So don't forget about your Sam
and I won't forget about you, Pam.

LIST WORDS

clause
figurative
foreshadow
indefinite
possessive
salutation
sequential
subordinate

Use Context as Clues to Meaning

Many terms that are related to writing have Latin roots. For example, the word *manuscript* has the Latin roots *manus* and *script*.

manus (hand) + script (to write) = manuscript (to write by hand)

The word *manuscript* usually refers to an author's original version of a text, even if he or she created that text on a computer.

Another word related to writing is *salutation,* which has the Latin root *salus,* meaning "good health." The opening section of a formal letter, the salutation, gets its name from the specific act of wishing someone good health. At the right are more words related to grammar, writing, and literature. You may come across these words in your language arts class.

Read the story below. How does the context help you understand the meanings of the underlined words?

Abbie stood at the entrance to the cave. She hugged her camera and flash close to her body, as if it might be snatched from her.

> Abbie sure sounds <u>possessive</u>! She is never letting go of that camera.

Something moving on the ground caught her attention. It was a huge, brown spider—a football with legs. She shuddered as an image of being trapped in a web came into her mind. She didn't like spiders.

> I like your use of <u>figurative</u> language, comparing the spider to a football.

> Good <u>foreshadowing</u>! This hint lets readers know that something is coming up in the story.

The spider scuttled ahead, and Abbie peered into the cave's darkness as it disappeared. She wiped the sweat from her forehead, made a face, and moved forward slowly. She tried to calm herself by thinking of the steps for turning on and focusing her camera.

> It would be nice to see this sentence rewritten to start with a <u>subordinate clause</u>, like "As Abbie peered into the cave's darkness, she saw the spider scuttle ahead and then disappear."

> For readers who don't know cameras, do you need to list the <u>sequential</u> steps for taking a picture?

She had walked a little ways into the cave when a giant spider at least twice her size appeared.

> The distance seems so <u>indefinite</u>. Should you add information on exactly how far Abbie walked before she reached the spider?

"Hello, Mr. Spider," she said. "I've been looking for you. Say cheese!"

> Isn't Abbie scared? Why would she offer the spider a <u>salutation</u>?

In Your Notebook Write each list word and its meaning. To check a meaning, use a dictionary.

Word Roots

Sequential is an adjective formed from the base word *sequence*. *Sequence* has the Latin root *sequi*, which means "to follow." Other words with this root are *sequel, consequence,* and *consecutive*. Prefixes and suffixes can be added to produce words such as *inconsequential* or *sequential*. These words have closely related meanings, but they are not the same. The series of the numbers five, six, and seven and the series of the numbers five, nine, and eleven are both sequential, but only the first series is consecutive.

Have you heard this expression?

The Latin phrase *non sequitur* contains the same root as *sequential—sequi*, which means "follow." *Non sequitur* means "it does not follow."

Apply and Extend

- In grammar, *subordinate clause* means "a dependent phrase." However, the words *subordinate* and *clause* have other general meanings as well. Write a sentence for each word, using the word's general meaning. You may want to consult a dictionary to check meanings.

- Sequential order is especially important when writing directions. Write directions for how to do or make something. Be sure that the sequential order of the directions is clear and correct. Exchange directions with a partner. Do you understand your partner's directions? Does your partner understand yours?

Skit Are you a good storyteller? Think about the words in this lesson. Work with a partner or small group to write and perform a skit that uses or is based on some of these words. For example, your skit might include hints that foreshadow the ending, or include a character who is possessive about something. It might take place at any time, in any location. Use your imagination, and have fun!

ceed, ced, cess

LIST 1

access
antecedent
concede
exceed
procedure
proceedings
secede
succession

Ceed is a Latin root that means "go." This root can also be spelled ***ced*** or ***cess***.

- Words containing *ceed, ced,* or *cess* usually have something to do with going or moving.
- Use *ceed, ced,* or *cess* as a clue to meaning when you come across words that contain this root.

ANCHOR WORD
pro**ceed**

When you see *ceed, ced,* or *cess,* think of ***proceed*** ("go" on after a stop or interruption).

Clues to Meaning Use *ceed, ced,* and *cess* as clues to the meanings of the underlined words.

Last year a succession of huge rainstorms hit our small town. It seemed we had a big storm every day for two weeks. The water in our river rose above the banks, exceeding what the river could hold. The floods overran our local streets, so we had no access to places like the grocery store near our house. We had water in our basement for days. First, we tried to fight it by using the following procedure: we would fill buckets and run outside to dump the water, and then we would run back inside and start all over again. We finally had to concede that the water was rising faster than we could bail it.

That was a terrible time, and when the water did recede, we were relieved. About a month later, our local paper published the proceedings of the town's most recent village board meeting. When we read those, we found out that the antecedent of the flooding was not only the storms but a giant buildup of leaves in our town sewer system. We couldn't believe that simply cleaning the town's sewer grates might have kept our basement dry. With that news, my family decided that we wanted to declare our independence and secede from our town!

LIST 2

proactive
procrastinate
project
projection

pro

Pro is a Latin prefix that means "forward" or "in front of."

- Words containing *pro* usually have something to do with moving forward or being in front of something.

When you see *pro,* think of ***propeller*** (device used to move boats and aircraft "forward").

Clues to Meaning Use *pro* as a clue to the meanings of the underlined words.

- Comedian Ellen DeGeneres once joked, "<u>Procrastinate</u> now; don't put it off until tomorrow."
- To <u>project</u> a positive image in the audition, Amber knew she had to be <u>proactive</u>, planning for every possible dance move they might ask her to perform.
- The shadow cast an eerie <u>projection</u> on the dense row of trees. "Is that a monster or a zombie?" wondered Russell nervously, as he spun around.

In Your Notebook Write each list word and a sentence that demonstrates its meaning.

Etymology Study

The word *etymology* comes from a Greek word, *etymologia,* which means "the original sense or form of a word." *Etymology* is the "explanation of the origin and history of a word." When you see word parts whose etymology you know, you can figure out what the word means. For example, in the following sentence, look at the underlined word.

Bella was <u>proactive</u> in planning the party and prepared all the food and decorations the day before.

You know that *pro* is a Latin prefix that means "forward" or "in front of." *Active* comes from the Latin word *actus,* which means "working, effective, in operation." Bella moved forward in her operations to get ready for the party.

Apply and Extend

List 1

If you exceed at something, you go beyond what is expected. Words related to *exceed* are *excess* and *excessive*. Use each word in a sentence.

List 1

Write a question about one of the words that contains *ceed, ced,* or cess, showing that you understand the meaning of the word. An example question for the word *access* is: *Which word means that someone has the right to go to an area?*

List 2

Write one sentence using as many of the list words as you can. Can you use all four words in the sentence? Challenge yourself!

Clue Review Play a word game with one of your classmates. Choose one of the list words. Give your partner a clue about the word. Did your partner guess the word correctly? If not, provide another clue until your partner correctly identifies the word. Then switch roles.

Did you know?

When used as words, *pro* means "for," and *con* means "against." The *pros* and *cons* of an issue are the arguments for and against it.

LIST WORDS

cranium
diffraction
diffusion
ligament
pelvis
refraction
retina
sternum

Use Context as Clues to Meaning

Diffraction, diffusion, and *refraction* are important concepts in the science of light, or optics. These nouns are made by adding the Latin suffix *ion* to verbs. The word *refraction* is related to the way we see. It means the change in direction from a wave or a ray of light.

The word *refraction* has the prefix *re,* the Latin root *fract,* and the suffix *ion.*

re (back) + fract (break) + ion (process of) = refraction
(the process of bending a ray or wave from a straight course)

At the left are more words related to optics and several related to anatomy, which is the science of the structure of living things. You may come across these words in your science class.

Read the following sentences. How does the context help you understand the meanings of the underlined words?

- Eight flat, sturdy bones make up your cranium, which protects your brain from injury.
- Diffraction, diffusion, and refraction all describe ways in which light acts. Light diffracts, or spreads out, when it passes through a narrow slit or past the sharp edge of an obstacle. When light hits some solid surfaces, it diffuses, or scatters. Refraction occurs when light moves from one substance to another, such as from air to water, and the angle of the light is bent.
- Without ligaments, or connecting tissue, your skeleton would fall apart.
- Your pelvis, which is between your abdomen and legs, is not just one bone, but many, including your tailbone.
- A tear in the delicate retina, which is a layer at the back of the eyeball, will affect your ability to see.
- Your ribs are attached to your breastbone, or sternum. Your sternum is a narrow, flat bone in the middle of your rib cage.

In Your Notebook Set up two columns with the heads "Optics" and "Anatomy." Write each list word in the appropriate column.

Using Online Reference Sources

How often have you had science homework that involved unfamiliar words? To find out more information about a word, such as longer descriptions and diagrams, use online references. Online references include books, websites, encyclopedias, and even scientific journals. To find reliable online resources, do the following:

- Type the term into a search engine.
- Choose search results from reliable sites, such as government agencies, universities, colleges, libraries, or museums. These sites' addresses end in *.gov, .edu,* or *.org*.
- You can also use online encyclopedias, such as *Britannica.com.* When in doubt, ask a librarian to recommend a source.

Have you heard this expression?

When we say "Hindsight is 20/20," we mean that when we look back at an experience or an event, we are able to see it clearly.

Apply and Extend

- *Diffraction, diffusion,* and *refraction* are nouns made from verbs with the added *ion* suffix. Choose one of these words. Write one sentence using the noun form and one sentence using the verb form.
- Most words form plurals by adding *s* or *es*. Latin words ending in *ium* or *um,* such as *cranium* and *sternum,* often form plurals by changing those endings to *ia* or *a*. Write the plurals of *cranium, ligament, pelvis, retina,* and *sternum*. Then choose one word. Write a sentence using the singular form and another using the plural form.

The Illustrated Word Sharpen your pencils—it's time to play a picture game. Divide a group into two teams. Write lesson words on cards and place them in a stack upside down. The first person on Team 1 takes a card, draws a picture that represents the word on the card, and shows the picture to his or her team. If team members guess the word in 30 seconds, the team gets a point. Now it's Team 2's turn.

LIST 1

postdate
postseason
postwar

post

Post is a Latin prefix that means "after."

- Words containing *post* usually have to do with something happening after.

When you see *post,* think of ***post****script* (an addition to a letter written "after" the letter is signed).

Clues to Meaning Use *post* as a clue to the meanings of the underlined words.

- In the postwar period following World War II, returning veterans needed homes.
- In postseason play, or games after regular-season games, the Giants won the World Series. These postdated games, which were played at a later date than regular-season games, were exciting to watch.

LIST 2

precedent
prefix
prehistoric
preposition

pre

Pre is a Latin prefix that when placed in front of a root or base word adds the meaning "before" to the word.

- Words containing *pre* have to do with something happening before or in advance.

When you see *pre,* think of ***pre****pay* (to pay "in advance").

Clues to Meaning Use *pre* as a clue to the meanings of the underlined words.

Cheryl I love crossword puzzles! The clue for 1 Across is "before events in history were written." I think the answer is prehistoric.

Jorge Right! The clue for 1 Down is "a word that expresses some relation to a noun, pronoun, phrase, or clause that follows it." Eleven letters—it must be preposition.

Cheryl Great! The clue for 3 Across is "comes before a base word to change its meaning or make another word." That's a prefix.

Jorge The clue for 3 Down is harder—"happens before and becomes an example for what happens later." I think the answer is precedent.

rect

LIST 3

correction
director
erect
rectangle
rectify

Rect is a Latin root that means "straight" or "right."

- Words containing *rect* usually have something to do with keeping something straight or right.

When you see *rect,* think of *direction* (a "straight" course).

Clues to Meaning Use *rect* as a clue to the meanings of the underlined words.

- Aggie sat straight, with erect posture, as she listened to the teacher explain that a rectangle is a shape that always has right angles.
- We chose Maya to be the director of the class play because she's talented at managing and guiding the actors.
- Erin checked her math homework for errors. She made corrections to rectify any inaccuracies.

In Your Notebook Write each list word and a clue to its meaning.

Analogy Study

An analogy shows a relationship between two pairs of words. The words in both word pairs are related in the same way. For example, the words may be antonyms. Antonyms are words with opposite meanings, such as *postseason* and *preseason*. Consider this analogy: *Postseason* is to *preseason* as *postwar* is to *prewar*.

Postseason means "after the season," and *preseason* means "before the season." *Postwar* means "after the war"; the opposite of *postwar* is *prewar*. The words in each pair are antonyms.

Apply and Extend

■ List 1

Write an analogy using one of the list words and three other words of your choice. The analogy may show antonyms, synonyms, or another relationship. If you need to do so, use a dictionary or go online to look for words.

Did you know?

Post hoc means "after this, as a result of this." It is a shortened form of the Latin *post hoc, ergo propter hoc,* which refers to a common misbelief that what comes before an event must also be its cause.

■ List 2

Write a sentence that includes one of the words in the list. Show that you understand the meaning by using an antonym to define the word in context.

■ List 3

Add two more words that have the root *rect* to the list words. Explain how the meaning of *rect* helps you figure out the meanings of these words.

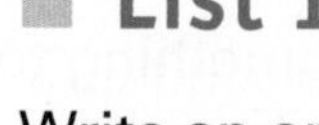

Word Part Invention How much of a wordsmith are you? With a partner, combine word parts from this lesson with other letters or syllables to invent a new word. Then write a definition for the word based on the meanings of the word parts. Share the word and definition with classmates.

LIST WORDS

assumption
credibility
evaluate
evidence
indictment
infraction
litigation
warrant

Use Context as Clues to Meaning

From lawbreakers to lawmakers and from criminals to judges, crime and justice are everywhere—in the news, books, and people's conversations. The words at the right are related to crime and justice. You may come across them in your social studies class.

Read this passage about crime and justice. How does the context help you understand the meanings of the underlined words?

Mrs. Emma Grant had some beautiful jewelry. And now it was time to take it to a jeweler who could evaluate it and tell her what it was worth. But when she gathered up her pieces, she discovered that a necklace was missing. Mrs. Grant contacted the police, who talked to her for a long time. Although they had no proof, the police believed that the thief was someone Mrs. Grant knew. On that assumption, they questioned Ms. Amanda Jones, Mrs. Grant's housekeeper. Ms. Jones denied the crime, but lost credibility because she kept changing her answers. The police didn't believe anything she said.

The police asked a judge to issue a warrant, or written order, that let them search Ms. Jones's home to look for evidence. They found the necklace immediately, which was certainly proof of the crime. Mrs. Grant knew that the police would charge Ms. Jones with an infraction, or violation, of the law, but she decided she would take legal action herself by filing litigation in court that accused Ms. Jones of stealing the necklace. However, she decided to wait until the district attorney went to court to file an indictment, or formal written accusation, against Ms. Jones. You could say that Ms. Jones wouldn't be wearing that necklace anytime soon!

In Your Notebook Write the list words. Beside each list word write the context clues in the passage that are provided for that word.

Suffix Study

When you add a suffix to a word, you form a new word that often is a different part of speech. For example, adding *ible* to the root *cred* (believe) forms an adjective, *credible* (believable). Adding the suffix *ibility* to the root *cred* forms the noun *credibility* (the fact or quality of being believable).

The word *indict* is a verb meaning "charge with an offense or crime." Adding the suffix *ment* forms the noun *indictment* meaning "a formal written accusation."

Did you know?

Testimony by people, objects, and documents are offered *into evidence* in a court of law to show or prove what is true and what is not true.

Apply and Extend

- *Assumption* is a noun made from a verb with the added *ion* suffix. *Evaluate* is a verb that can be turned into a noun by adding *ion*. Choose one of these words. Write one sentence using the noun form and one sentence using the verb form.
- The word *warrant* has general meanings beyond its meaning in social studies. Write two sentences, each using a different meaning of *warrant*. Use context to show you understand both meanings.

Graphic Gallery Use your skills as a cartoonist to create a comic strip using words from this week's lesson. Draw pictures and write dialogue or use an online program to create the graphic text. How many of the words can you use? Work together with classmates to compile the class's comic strips into a Graphic Gallery.

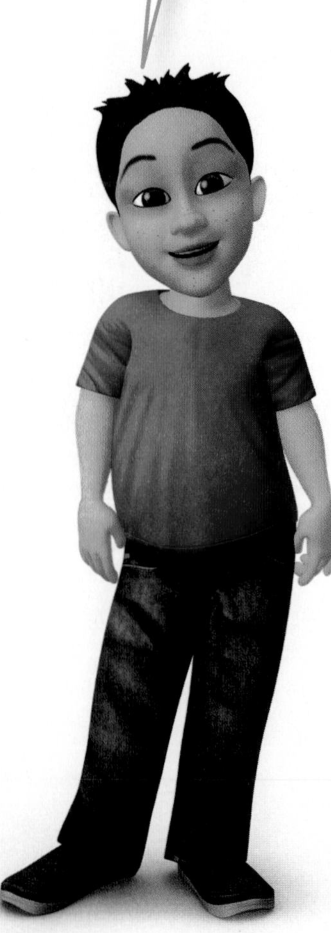

gress — LIST 1

aggression
Congress
progressive
regress
transgress
transgressor

Gress is a Latin root that means "go" or "step."

- The word *progress* has a Latin prefix and Latin root.

pro (forward) + gress (go) = progress

ANCHOR WORD: pro**gress**

When you see *gress,* think of *pro**gress*** ("go" forward or "step" ahead).

Clues to Meaning Use *gress* as a clue to the meanings of the underlined words.

- The driver was always careful to follow the law and not <u>transgress</u>.
- The dog was friendly with his owner, but showed <u>aggression</u> with strangers. He barked and bared his teeth if a stranger got too close.
- The <u>progressive</u> town was constantly improving its services. It vowed to never <u>regress</u> to what it had been years ago.
- Because of her background in law and her interest in politics, she ran for a seat in <u>Congress</u> to represent her state.
- After prison, the <u>transgressor</u> decided never to break the law again.

re — LIST 2

repression
retraction
reversible

Re is a Latin prefix that means "back."

- Words containing *re* usually have something to do with going back or taking something back.

ANCHOR WORD: **re**verse

When you see *re,* think of ***re**verse* (turn "back").

Clues to Meaning Use *re* as a clue to the meanings of the underlined words.

In its latest <u>repression</u> of the truth, the blog printed a false report about the mayor. It later printed a <u>retraction</u> of the report, but the damage done was not <u>reversible</u>. The mayor lost his reelection.

LIST 3

retroactive
retrograde
retrospect

retro

Retro is a Latin prefix that means "backward."

- The word *retrogress* has a Latin prefix and a Latin root.

retro (backward) + gress (go) = retrogress

When you see *retro* think of ***retro**gress* (go "backward").

Clues to Meaning Use *retro* as a clue to the meanings of the underlined words.

- In <u>retrospect</u>, as we look back, we wish we would've practiced more so that we didn't come in last place at the volleyball tournament.
- In August, Corey's boss gave him a <u>retroactive</u> pay increase, which should have taken effect two months before.
- Sparky's training was going well until he chewed his owner's shoes. To go back on the progress that he made was a <u>retrograde</u> step.

In Your Notebook Write each list word and another form of it, such as *aggression/aggress*. For one pair, write a sentence for each word.

Mythological Allusions

Sometimes to make a point, a writer will make a mythological allusion, using a term that refers to a story in mythology. For example, a "Herculean task" is a mythological allusion. It refers to Hercules, a hero of Greek mythology. You learned that *transgress* means "to break a rule or a law." Hercules committed a transgression: he had murdered his wife and child while under an evil spell. To make amends for his wrongdoing, he had to complete twelve impossible labors. He finished them, was forgiven, and became a hero. Today a Herculean task means a "huge, difficult task."

Apply and Extend

List 1

Work with a partner. Choose a word and write a "What if" question, such as *What if someone shows aggression at a party?* Answer each other's question. An answer to this question might be *People will avoid a person who shows aggression.*

List 2

Write a riddle using two words that begin with the prefix *re*. An example is: *If a cat draws its claws back in, is that a retraction or repression of its claws?* Answer your riddle.

List 3

Find one more word with the prefix *retro*. Write a sentence using your new word and one or two list words. Provide context that shows that you understand the meanings of the words.

Did you know?

The stand-alone word *retro* means a revived style. It is often used to refer to fashion or design that takes its inspiration from the past.

Word History Choose an interesting word from this week's lesson. What can you find out about the history and origins of your word? Answer the following questions:

- From which language did your word derive?
- What is the first recorded instance of its use in the English language?
- What is one interesting fact you learned about the word?
- List related words that you find.

LIST WORDS

divisor
estimate
hypotenuse
isosceles
minuend
numerator
quotient
scalene

Use Context as Clues to Meaning

Mathematics concepts are progressive, which means that you will learn terms that build on what you already know. Mathematics may deal in numbers, but its concepts can be described in words. For example, the word *isosceles* has the Greek words *isos* meaning "equal" and *sceles* meaning "leg." An isosceles triangle has two "legs," or sides, that are of equal length. At the left are more words related to math. You may come across these words in your math class.

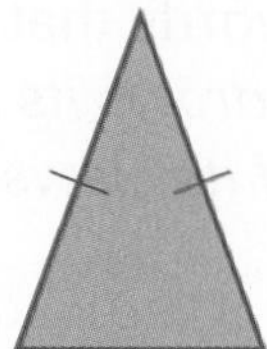

isosceles triangle

Read the following information about math. How does the context help you understand the meanings of the underlined words?

- To add or subtract large numbers, first estimate, or roughly calculate, the answer. Then solve the problem.
- In 16 ÷ 2 = 8, 16 is the dividend, 2 is the divisor, and 8 is the quotient.
- In 50 – 26 = 24, 50 is the minuend, 26 is the subtrahend, and 24 is the remainder.
- In the fraction $\frac{1}{2}$, 1 is the numerator and 2 is the denominator.
- Unlike an isosceles triangle, which has two sides of equal length, a scalene triangle has three sides of unequal length. In a right triangle, the hypotenuse is the longest side opposite the 90° angle.

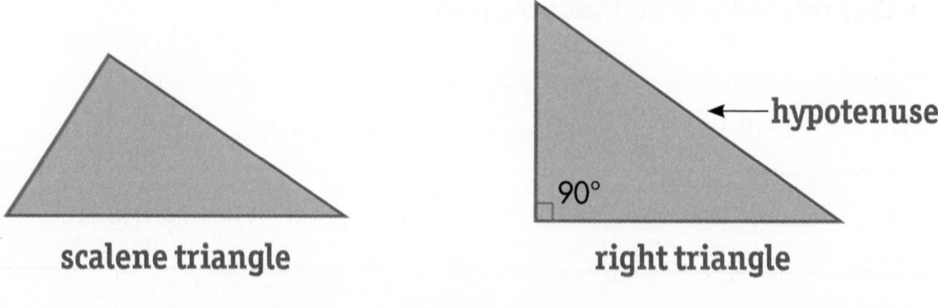

scalene triangle   right triangle

In Your Notebook Write each list word and its meaning. If possible, use an illustration to define the word.

Etymology Study

Knowing the etymology, or origin, of a math word might help you solve a math problem. For example, *minuend* shares a Latin root with *minus,* meaning "to make smaller." So, in the equation 50 – 26 = 24, which number is to be made smaller? 50 is the *minuend*.

And which side of a right triangle is its *hypotenuse? Hypo* is Greek for "under," and *tenuse* comes from the Greek for "to stretch." So, remember that the *hypotenuse* is the leg of a right triangle that "stretches under" its 90° angle.

One way to solve a word problem in math is to start by breaking down words into their parts. Think about the meaning of the words and then work on solving the problem.

Did you know?

Numerator, numerous, and *innumerable* share the Latin root *numerus. Numerous* means "a large number" while *innumerable* means "too many to count."

Apply and Extend

- The word *estimate* can be used as both a noun and a verb. Write one sentence using the noun form and one using the verb form. Include context to show you understand the meaning of the words. Show your sentences to a partner. Have your partner identify how you used *estimate* in each sentence.
- The word *numerator* comes from the Latin root *numerus,* meaning "number." Look up the meanings of *numerator, numerous,* and *innumerable.* Write two or three sentences to explain how the prefixes and suffixes change the meaning of each word.

Clue Review Play a word game with one of your classmates. Choose one of the list words. Give your partner a clue about the word. Did your partner guess the word correctly? If not, provide another clue until your partner correctly identifies the word. Then switch roles.

LESSON 21 Word Parts and Meanings

fac, fec, fic, fy, ex, e

LIST 1 fac, fec, fic, fy

artifact
artificial
facsimile
falsify
ineffective
infection
personify
proficient

Fac is a Latin root that means "make." Other ways to spell this root are ***fec, fic,*** and ***fy***.

- Words containing *fac, fec, fic,* or *fy* usually have something to do with making something or something made.

When you see *fac, fec, fic,* or *fy,* think of ***fac****tory* (a place where something is "made").

Clues to Meaning Use *fac, fec, fic,* and *fy* as clues to the meanings of the underlined words.

- In 2009, a metal detector enthusiast discovered the largest collection of Anglo-Saxon gold ever found. The man-made artifacts date to about A.D. 650.
- If you are missing an arm or leg, you can replace it with an artificial limb made from metal and plastic. It can help you do daily activities.
- The museum staff made a facsimile, or copy, of the bracelet to put on display so the real one would not be lost or stolen.
- "Your efforts to make peace with your sister have been ineffective," Mom said. "All of that talking, and you're still not getting along!"
- The basketball coach told him to spend more time making free throws so he could become a proficient player. "You'll never get to be an expert without practice," said the coach.
- The attorney asked the businessman if he had tried to falsify his tax records. The man replied that he would never provide untrue information to the government.
- My brother said that Jackie Robinson had come to personify baseball for him. Whenever he thought of the sport, he thought of this historic baseball player.
- The nurse looked at the rash on his hand. "That's a bad infection," she said. "You'll need a strong ointment to heal it."

ex, e

LIST 2

egress
emergent
exclusion
exile

Ex is a Latin prefix that means "out." Another way to spell this root is ***e***.

- Words containing *ex* or *e* usually have something to do with going out of or away from.

When you see *ex* or *e,* think of ***exit*** (the way "out").

Clues to Meaning Use *ex* and *e* as clues to the meanings of the underlined words.

- The police stopped the crowd and prevented their egress by announcing that no one would be allowed to leave the building.
- The emergent sun brightened my mood as it rose.
- The 19th Amendment gave women the right to vote. There would no longer be any exclusion of women from the voting booth.
- After stepping down from the throne, Napoleon Bonaparte was sent to live in exile, away from his home country, on the island of Elba.

In Your Notebook Use each list word in a sentence that contains context clues to the word's meaning.

Synonym Study

To move people through his sideshow quickly, P. T. Barnum, the founder of the Ringling Bros. and Barnum & Bailey Circus, put up a sign, "This way to the egress." People followed, thinking they were about to see something exciting. Instead, they found themselves on the street. *Egress* and *exit* are synonyms. Here are some more synonyms:

- A synonym for *ineffective* is *feckless.*
- A synonym for *personify* is *embody.*
- Two synonyms for *exile* are *banish* and *banishment,* depending on whether *exile* is used as a noun or as a verb.

Synonyms can make what you read and write much more interesting.

Apply and Extend

List 1

The words *artificial* and *facsimile* have different meanings but are similar in their meanings too. Tell how the words are alike. Then write a sentence for each word that shows how these words are different.

Did you know?
Sending a fax is a quick way to send information electronically. *Fax* is short for *facsimile*, which comes from Latin words that mean "to make" and "similar."

List 1

Write a question about one of the words in List 1, showing that you understand its meaning. An example question for the word *proficient* is: *Which word describes someone who is skilled or expert at doing something?*

List 2

Write one sentence using as many of the list words as you can. Challenge yourself. Can you use all four words in one sentence?

Word Part Invention How much of a wordsmith are you? With a partner, combine word parts from this lesson with other letters or syllables to invent a new word. Then write a definition for the word based on the meanings of the word parts. Share the word and definition with classmates.

LIST WORDS

affiliation
ally
commune
confederation
consensus
dispute
faction
kinship

Use Context as Clues to Meaning

If you were talking or writing about *communities,* you might use words in this lesson. The word *community* comes from the Latin word *communem,* which means "common." *Community* has the prefix *com,* which means "with," and the root *mun,* which means "duty." To belong to a community is to share a duty or responsibility with other people.

A *faction* is a group of persons within a larger community acting together or having a common purpose. The word *faction,* which has the Latin root *fac,* meaning "make" or "do," comes from a Latin word that means "party" or "class." A faction is a community of persons who join together to do something.

Read the paragraphs below. How does the context help you understand the meanings of the underlined words?

Conflict can threaten a community, but it can also create one. Say a dispute, or disagreement, arises in a community between one faction, or part of the group, whose members hold one opinion and a different faction whose members hold a different opinion. They may try to reach consensus by discussing their differences and trying to develop a plan that everyone can agree to. If they are unable to settle their differences, the two factions may split into two new communities. Even people who do not have an affiliation with one side or the other may have to join a side.

When conflicts arise among individuals, groups, or nations, one may become the ally of another. They may agree to be friends and to defend each other while respecting each other's independence. Sometimes people join together, or unite, in this way to form a confederation.

Kinship communities are not voluntary. You can choose your friends, but you can't choose the people in your family. A commune is like a voluntary kinship community. Members live in some ways like a family, but they do so by choice.

In Your Notebook Write the list words. Then choose two words and make a 4-square concept map for each word.

Using an Online Thesaurus

Synonyms are good context clues to an unfamiliar word's meaning. They can also make your writing clearer and give it style. To find synonyms quickly, use an online thesaurus. But what do you do when you need a synonym for a word with different nuances of meaning?

In an online thesaurus, each meaning of a word has its own set of synonyms. You may see a list of meanings for the word to choose from. Once you find the meaning that you are looking for, you can scroll down or link to the synonyms that go with that meaning.

For example, the word *community* has several different meanings, such as "society of people," "brotherhood," and "civilization." The list of synonyms for each of these meanings will be different. You must first determine which meaning or nuance of the word you want to use in order to find an accurate synonym.

Do you know these expressions?

- political affiliation
- political ally
- ally yourself with someone
- come to a consensus

Apply and Extend

- Explain how *consensus, confederation,* and *affiliation* have something to do with being united.
- Look up the word *commune* in a dictionary. Write two different definitions for the word. Then, look up the word in an online thesaurus. Write three synonyms for each meaning of *commune*.

Word History Choose an interesting word from this week's lesson. Answer the following questions:

- From which language did your word derive?
- What is the first recorded instance of its use in the English language?
- What is one interesting fact you learned about the word?
- List related words that you find.

bene — LIST 1

benefactor
beneficial
beneficiary
benevolent

Bene is a Latin root that means "good" or "well."

- Words containing *bene* are usually related to doing something good.
- Use *bene* as a clue to meaning when you come across words that contain this root.

ANCHOR WORD **bene**fit

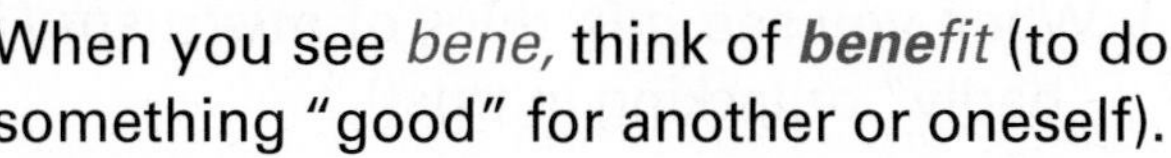

When you see *bene,* think of ***bene****fit* (to do something "good" for another or oneself).

Clues to Meaning Use *bene* as a clue to the meanings of the underlined words.

- The benevolent, or well-meaning, millionaire made the college a beneficiary of his will, leaving all of his money to that school.
- "Thank you for being my benefactor by supporting my dog-sitting business," Carla said to her neighbor. "Telling your friends about me has been very helpful and beneficial in getting new customers."

mal — LIST 2

malady
malicious
malign
malnourished

Mal is a Latin root that means "bad."

- The word *malfunction* has two Latin roots.

mal (bad) + function (perform) = malfunction

ANCHOR WORD **mal**function

When you see *mal,* think of ***mal****function* (functioning or performing "badly").

Clues to Meaning Use *mal* as a clue to the meanings of the underlined words.

- "Have you ever seen such malicious, nasty behavior?" cried Kim to other students at the car wash after Patrick threw a sponge at a customer. "He constantly insults and maligns customers, so they drive away."
- With so little to eat, the poor children suffered from symptoms of a common malady caused by bad nutrition. What food they have had is so unhealthful that they've been malnourished for many months.

LIST 3

mis

mischievous
miscue
misgiving
misnomer

Mis is an Old English prefix that means "badly" or "wrongly."

- To figure out words with the prefix *mis,* identify the root or base word first and then add the meaning "badly" or "wrongly."

When you see *mis,* think of ***mis****trustful* (trusting "badly" or lacking in trust).

Clues to Meaning Use *mis* as a clue to the meanings of the underlined words.

When Tina asked me to join the Problem Pals, I had misgivings about what the group was about. I had my doubts until I found out that calling it Problem Pals is a misnomer. The name misrepresents the club. I think whoever named the club was probably a little playful and mischievous. I certainly miscued because of the name. Club members agree to secretly do nice things for people, such as finding something a person has lost. I told the club that changing the name would keep potential members from misinterpreting their purpose.

In Your Notebook Write the list words. Then choose two words and make a 4-square concept map for each word.

Connotation and Denotation

A word's denotation is its literal, dictionary definition. A word's connotation is the meaning, associations, or emotions that it suggests or implies. Connotations can be either positive or negative. For example, the word *slender* has a positive connotation, while the word *scrawny* has a negative connotation because it suggests an unattractive appearance.

The word *malicious* also has a negative connotation. It suggests that someone wishes to cause harm or suffering. The word *mischievous*, on the other hand, has a more positive connotation. It implies that someone causes trouble in a playful way.

As a writer, why is it important to think about connotation and denotation?

Apply and Extend

List 1

Think about how *benefactor, benevolent,* and *beneficiary* are related in meaning. How is a benefactor benevolent to a beneficiary? Write a sentence or two using these three words.

List 2

Write a question about one of the words that contains *mal,* showing that you understand the meaning of the word. An example question for the word *malicious* is: *Which word describes a person who spreads nasty, false rumors about other people?*

List 3

The prefix *mis* may change the meaning of a word to its opposite. For example, a *fortune* is a good thing, but a *misfortune* is a lack of fortune or luck. Did you notice the words *misrepresents* and *misinterpreting* in the passage? What do they mean? Can you think of two other words with the prefix *mis* that change the base word to its opposite?

Rap It Up Working with a classmate, choose a word from the week's lesson. Use the word and its definition to create a short poem or rap. Compile your rap with other classmates' raps into a Rap It Up notebook.

Did you know?

The word *malaria* (*mal* = bad and *aria* = air) first described a disease thought to be caused by "bad air" in swampy areas. Today, we know that an infected mosquito causes malaria.

LIST WORDS

acknowledgment
copyright
cross-reference
document
editorial
periodical
plagiarism
preface

Use Context as Clues to Meaning

The world of language arts is filled with millions of words, many of which are related, such as *benefit, beneficial,* and *beneficiary.* Likewise, the word *editor* is related to *editorial.* Have you ever read an editorial? Perhaps you've even written one for your school blog. At the left are more words related to language arts. You may come across these words in your language arts class.

Read this description of a language arts class. How does the context help you understand the meanings of the underlined words?

You will be reading many different types of documents this year, such as letters, books, and short stories. You will also be reading articles in newspapers and periodicals, or magazines published monthly or weekly. Some of the articles will be editorials, which give the editor's opinion on an issue. Documents often include features that contain useful information. For example, the copyright information, found near the front of a book or periodical, tells you the title, author, publisher, and the date when the material was published.

To include something in your writing that you have read, name the author and source of the information. This will help you avoid plagiarism, or stealing the words and ideas of others.

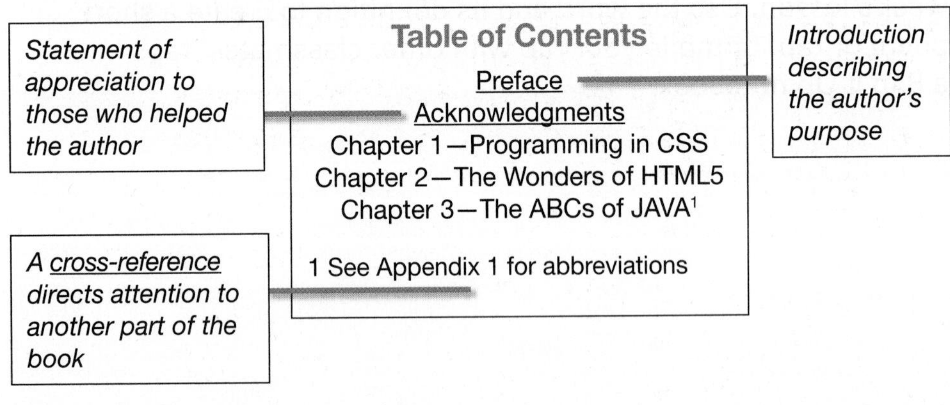

In Your Notebook Write each underlined list word and its meaning. To check a meaning, use a dictionary.

Context Clues

The words before or after an unfamiliar word often help you figure out its meaning. Look for clues such as descriptions, examples, or even definitions. For example, in the passage on the previous page, the word *documents* is followed by examples—letters, books, short stories, and so on. What do those examples have in common? Documents must be something written or printed.

Apply and Extend

- The word *preface* has several meanings. In this lesson, *preface* refers to a section at the beginning of a book. What other meanings do you know? Use *preface* in a sentence, demonstrating a different meaning for the word. You may want to use a dictionary to check the meaning.
- The sentence, *The publisher made several editorial changes to the editorial,* uses the word *editorial* as both an adjective and a noun. Similarly, the word *document* can be used as a noun or a verb. Write a sentence using *document* as both a noun and verb.

Skit You are in charge of putting together a book containing original poems, stories, songs, and artwork created by your classmates. Work with several classmates to write and perform a skit about planning the parts of the book. Use as many words from this lesson as possible in your skit.

Did you know?

The word *plagiarism* comes from a Latin word meaning "kidnapper." Today, the word is used to describe a "literary kidnapper"—someone who steals the words and ideas of others.

LESSON 25 Word Parts and Meanings

ven, vent, circum

LIST 1

event
intervene
invention
preventable
revenue
venture

ven, vent

Ven is a Latin root that means "come." Another way to spell this root is ***vent***.

- Words containing *ven* or *vent* usually have something to do with something coming.

ANCHOR WORD: con**ven**tion

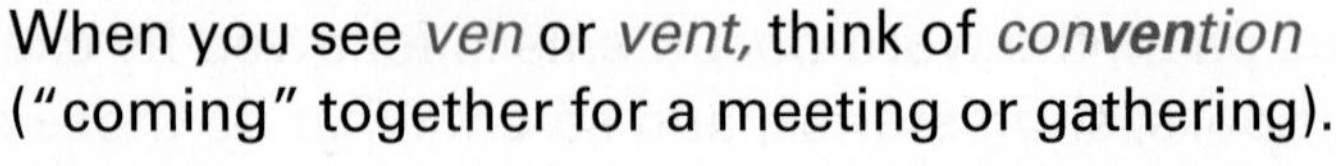

When you see *ven* or *vent,* think of ***convention*** ("coming" together for a meeting or gathering).

Clues to Meaning Use *ven* and *vent* as clues to the meanings of the underlined words.

- The convention was a yearly event—a happening that Derek didn't want to miss. As he rushed there on his bike, a car got too close and Derek fell. He was fine, but his bike wasn't. This gave him an idea for an invention, a brand-new item no one had ever made: a little box for cars that would sound an alarm when someone got too close to the car. He would call it the Preventable Pro—"preventable" because it would stop accidents. The revenue, or money people would pay for it, would buy Derek a brand new bike.
- Milo wanted to venture deep into the forest, off the trail, but Lisa thought it was too risky. Milo was upset that his sister always played it safe. Seeing the two teens argue, a park ranger intervened to explain why the paths were the safest places to explore the forest.

LIST 2

hyperventilate
ventilation

vent

Vent is a Latin root that means "wind."

- Words containing *vent* usually have something to do with wind.

ANCHOR WORD: vent

When you see *vent,* think of ***vent*** (a hole or opening that serves as an outlet for something such as "wind").

Clues to Meaning Use *vent* as a clue to the meanings of the underlined words.

"Open the window! I need fresh air!" Hilary demanded. "I'm starting to hyperventilate," she said as her breathing became quick.

"You need to relax," Marta said calmly, "and you don't need to breathe in so much air! This car's ventilation allows air to circulate even with the windows closed."

circum

LIST 3

circumnavigate
circumspect
circumstance
circumvent

Circum is a Latin prefix that means "around."

- To figure out words with the prefix *circum,* identify the root or base word first and then add the meaning "around."

When you see *circum,* think of ***circum****ference* (the distance "around").

Clues to Meaning Use *circum* as a clue to the meanings of the underlined words.

In 1519, Ferdinand Magellan bravely set out from Spain to circumnavigate, or sail around, the globe. A more circumspect captain might have been too careful to do it. Magellan and his crew had troubles, which threatened to circumvent the voyage and stop the trip. The circumstances, or events, of his death are known: in 1521, he was killed in a battle with islanders in the Philippines.

In Your Notebook Write each list word and a brief clue that will help you remember the word.

Using a Thesaurus

Use a thesaurus to find synonyms, or words with similar meanings that have slightly different connotations, or implied meanings. A thesaurus can help you find the exact word you need to make your writing precise and vivid. For example, to find a colorful word for being careful, look up *careful.* You may find *cautious, vigilant, wary, prudent,* and *circumspect.* To choose the synonym that best matches the context of your writing, look up its exact meaning in a dictionary.

Apply and Extend

Have you heard these expressions?

- Necessity is the mother of invention.
- Nothing ventured, nothing gained.
- under the circumstances

List 1

Choose two words in the list. For each, write a related word and its meaning. For *event,* you might write *eventual,* meaning "coming in the end," or *eventful,* meaning "full of events."

List 2

The words *ventilation* and *ventilator* are related. A *ventilator* is a machine for improving the quality of the air in an enclosed space. How are *ventilation* and *ventilator* related to the root *vent?*

List 3

The word *circumstance* has several meanings. Write two sentences, each using a different meaning of *circumstance.* Use context to show you understand both meanings.

Clue Review Play a word game with one of your classmates. Choose one of the list words. Give your partner a clue about the word. Did your partner guess the word correctly? If not, provide another clue until your partner correctly identifies the word. Then switch roles.

LIST WORDS

capillary
deplete
enzyme
excretion
hormone
nutrient
plasma
replenish

Use Context as Clues to Meaning

Have you ever felt out of breath after running for a long time? You might need to move inside to a place with good ventilation to help you replenish the air in your lungs.

The word *replenish* has a Latin prefix and root. *Re* is a prefix that means "again."

re (again) + plenus (full) = replenish (fill again)

The Latin root *plenus* means "full." *Replenish* means "fill again" or "provide a new supply for." When you have exercised for a long period of time, you may need to eat or to get a supply of fresh air to *replenish* your energy. At the right are more words related to the human body. You may come across these words in your science class.

Read about digestion and the circulatory system. How does the context help you understand the meanings of the underlined words?

What is going on? Your energy level is low, and your strength and vitality are drained, or depleted. Your body craves food to replenish, or restore, the nutrients it has used so you can continue to grow and be healthy. You have pangs of hunger, so you eat. Afterward your body releases enzymes, which cause or speed up changes in your body. The enzyme pepsin starts the process of digestion by breaking down food.

Your circulatory system is an important part of the digestive process. Blood vessels called capillaries have slender openings that join an artery to a vein and allow nutrients and waste products to pass through your digestive system. Your circulatory system also helps transfer hormones that control the activity of organs or tissues. For example, insulin is a hormone that regulates the sugar in your body. Plasma is the liquid part of the blood that transfers nutrients to the organs and waste products to the kidneys, liver, and lungs for elimination, or excretion.

In Your Notebook Write each list word and briefly tell what role it plays in keeping your body healthy. An example sentence for the word *enzyme* is: *An enzyme starts or speeds up changes in the body to help it work the way it should.*

Word Story

The word *juice* may call up an image of a glass of orange juice or a rare, juicy steak, but it also refers to fluid in the body. Gastric juices in the stomach help to digest food.

The words *juice* and *enzyme* both come from the Greek *zyme,* which means "leaven." A substance that will cause a change, such as yeast that causes bread to rise, is a leaven. Here's the origin of *enzyme.*

en (into) + zyme (leaven) = enzyme (a substance produced in living cells that is able to cause or speed up changes in other substances and not be changed itself)

Did you know?

Plasma is a component of human blood, but *plasma* is also the name of a gas used in electronics. A plasma TV is a very thin, flat-screen television that uses plasma cells to create a picture.

Apply and Extend

- The words *plasma* and *capillaries* are used in discussing the way blood circulates through the body. Write a sentence for each word, explaining how the word relates to the circulation of blood.
- The words *deplete* and *replenish* have general meanings in addition to their use in science. Write one sentence to show the general meaning of each word. An example sentence for *replenish* is: *The bookstore had to replenish its supply of T-shirts with logos after our team went to the playoffs.*

Clue Review Play a word game with one of your classmates. Choose one of the list words. Give your partner a clue about the word. Did your partner guess the word correctly? If not, provide another clue until your partner correctly identifies the word. Then switch roles.

man

LIST 1

maneuver
manipulate
manual
manufacture

Man is a Latin root that means "hand."

- Words containing *man* usually have something to do with the hands.

When you see *man,* think of ***man**icure* (care for the fingernails and "hands").

Clues to Meaning Use *man* as a clue to the meanings of the underlined words.

- Use a mouse to <u>maneuver</u> around the Internet, moving from website to website. Beware of pictures. Anyone with a camera phone can <u>manufacture</u>, or make, a false image or video and put it online.
- <u>Manual</u> labor is work done with the hands, not with machines. Gardening and construction are <u>manual</u> labor.
- The pilot <u>manipulated</u> the controls of the plane for takeoff, flipping all of the switches with both hands.

ped

LIST 2

centipede
pedestal
pedestrian
pedicure
pedometer

Ped is a Latin root that means "foot."

- Words containing *ped* usually have something to do with the feet.

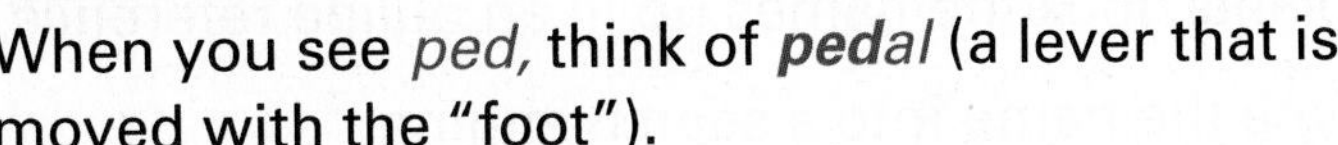

When you see *ped,* think of ***ped**al* (a lever that is moved with the "foot").

Clues to Meaning Use *ped* as a clue to the meanings of the underlined words.

- A <u>centipede</u> is a wormlike animal without a backbone, but with many legs. It might have as few as 28 legs or as many as 354.
- According to my <u>pedometer</u>, I walked 5,000 steps, or 2.5 miles.
- On August 22, 1886, workers completed the <u>pedestal</u> on which the Statue of Liberty would stand.
- Perhaps the world's busiest <u>pedestrian</u> crossing is in Tokyo, Japan, where as many as 2,500 people cross the street at once.
- Most <u>pedicures</u> include a foot soak, nail trim, and nail polish.

LIST 3

arthropod
podiatrist
podium

pod

Pod is a Greek root that means "foot."

- Words containing *pod* usually have something to do with the feet.
- When you see *pod,* think of *tri**pod*** (something with three "legs").

Clues to Meaning Use *pod* as a clue to the meanings of the underlined words.

In her nightmare, Sara steps up to a podium to deliver her speech. She realizes the room is full of podiatrists at their annual convention. She panics. "I don't know anything about foot doctors! My speech is about arthropods, you know, animals without backbones, with jointed bodies and legs. I thought this was an insect convention!"

In Your Notebook Write each list word and its meaning. Draw sketches for any words that you can.

Online Reference Sources

Scientists use Latin and Greek words to name all living things. To understand the meanings of the Latin and Greek names of animals and plants, look the names up in an online reference source.

- Type the name into a search engine.
- Choose reliable websites, such as universities (.edu), zoological societies (.org), or the government (.gov).
- Take notes and check your information in at least two sources.

Apply and Extend

List 1

Maneuver and *manipulate* both have to do with movement. Both words also have multiple meanings. Choose one of these words. Write two or three sentences that show the different meanings of the word.

List 2

Think about how *pedestal, pedestrian,* and *pedicure* are related in meaning. Could you find a pedestrian on a pedestal? Can a pedestrian have a pedicure? Write a sentence or two, using these three words.

List 3

Write a riddle for one of the words. For example, a riddle for *podiatrist* is: *Which word would be really interested in your feet?* Share your riddle with a partner and have your partner try to solve it.

Word Part Invention How much of a wordsmith are you? With a partner, combine word parts from this lesson with other letters or syllables to invent a new word. Then write a definition for the word based on the meanings of the word parts. Share the word and definition with classmates.

Have you heard these expressions?

- put on a pedestal
- How pedestrian!
- manual labor

LIST WORDS

autonomous
citizen
communism
despot
diplomat
fascism
nationalism
patriotism

Use Context as Clues to Meaning

One type of social science is political science. In political science, you analyze how governments are organized and how they work. For example, some nations are autonomous—they have their own government and rule themselves.

The word *autonomous* has two Greek roots, *auto* and *nomos.*

auto (self) + nomos (law) = autonomous (self-governing)

At the left are more words related to political science. You may come across these words in your social studies class.

Read the following sentences about political science. How does the context help you understand the meanings of the underlined words?

- The U.S. government recognizes 565 autonomous, or self-governing, Native American tribes.
- While communism in its purest form may sound like a fair economic and social system, it is difficult to make sure that all of a country's citizens, or members, share equally in the country's wealth.
- Fascism is a system of government that is usually headed by a dictator who has absolute control over the government. Despots are dictators who rule in a cruel and harsh way.
- In fascism, people are expected to display a fierce nationalism, openly showing their strong support for their leader and country.
- Someone who loves his or her country feels a strong sense of patriotism. Some patriotic citizens become government workers, such as diplomats, who manage relationships between their country and other nations.

In Your Notebook Write the list words. Next to each word, write the context clue or clues that helped you figure out the word's meaning.

Suffix Study

Ism is an interesting Greek suffix. It can be added to certain nouns, adjectives, and verbs to create a noun that means:

- "a belief system" such as Buddhism
- "a practice of" such as baptism
- "a quality of" such as patriotism

Communism, fascism, socialism, and nationalism are all political isms. Some isms are discriminatory beliefs, such as racism, ageism, and sexism.

Ism can also be a stand-alone word. It means a distinctive doctrine or belief. *Those students are learning about communism and socialism. What isms are you interested in learning about?*

Did you know?

While a country's diplomat is a person who manages relationships with other countries, the word *diplomat* is also used to describe, simply, a person who has skill in dealing with other people.

Apply and Extend

- *Citizen, dictator,* and *diplomat* are nouns that identify individuals. For each word, make up a character and write a sentence that conveys something about what he or she believes.
- Write two or three sentences that describe how you feel about patriotism.

Word History Choose an interesting word from this week's lesson. What can you find out about the history and origins of your word? Answer the following questions:

- From which language did your word derive?
- What is the first recorded instance of its use in the English language?
- What is one interesting fact you learned about the word?
- List related words that you find.

LIST 1

cosmic
cosmonaut
cosmopolitan
microcosm

cosm

Cosm is a Greek root that means "universe" or "world."

- Words containing *cosm* usually have something to do with the whole world or the entire universe.

When you see *cosm,* think of ***cosmos*** (the entire "universe").

Clues to Meaning Use *cosm* as a clue to the meanings of the underlined words.

- Cosmic rays are high-energy particles that strike Earth from space.
- In 1961, Yuri Gagarin, a Soviet cosmonaut, was the first person to visit space. He orbited the Earth one time in the spaceship *Vostok* 1.
- My grandmother was very cosmopolitan. She visited every continent, lived in different countries, and learned several languages.
- A big U.S. city is a microcosm of the whole world. Its neighborhoods are like different countries, with different languages and cultures.

LIST 2

geodesic
geology
geometric
geopolitical

geo

Geo is a Greek root that means "Earth."

- Words containing *geo* often have something to do with the Earth.

When you see *geo,* think of ***geography*** (the study of "Earth's" surface, climate, continents, countries, peoples, industries, and products).

Clues to Meaning Use *geo* as a clue to the meanings of the underlined words.

- A geodesic building is curved like the top half of the Earth.
- In geology, you learn about the materials that make up Earth.
- Erin loved the geometric look of the building—the steel beams on the building's outer walls formed triangles up and down its sides.
- The geopolitical importance of the river was undeniable. Leaders of neighboring countries discussed sharing the river for shipping.

ob, op

LIST 3

- obligation
- obstacle
- obstruction
- oppression

Ob is a Latin prefix with many meanings. Two meanings are "toward" or "against." Another way to spell this prefix is ***op***.

- Words with the prefix *ob* or *op* often mean going toward or against something.

When you see *ob* or *op,* think of ***ob****ject* (noun: something "toward" which action is directed; verb: give a reason "against").

Clues to Meaning Use *ob* and *op* as clues to the meanings of the underlined words.

- I feel an obligation to attend the concert. I promised my friend I would hear him play trumpet; I feel that I need to keep my word.
- As a child, he had to overcome asthma, an obstacle to becoming a trumpet player, which requires deep breathing.
- Another obstruction to his joining the band was that other members thought he might not keep up, but he showed he could.
- He likes to play dramatic, moving music that tells stories of sadness and oppression, about people suffering because of unjust treatment.

In Your Notebook Use each list word in a sentence that contains context clues to the word's meaning.

Antonym Study

An antonym is a word that has the opposite meaning of another word. The list word *cosmopolitan* means "feeling at home in all parts of the world." Its antonyms include *unworldly* and *provincial.* Like *cosmopolitan,* the list word *cosmic* uses the root *cosm,* which means "universe" or "world." *Cosmic* means "having to do with the whole universe." Its antonyms, therefore, would have the opposite meaning. Words such as *tiny* and *miniscule* are antonyms for *cosmic.*

Can you find antonyms for any other list words?

Apply and Extend

Have you heard these expressions?

- obstacle course
- under obligation
- moral obligation

List 1

Look up the meaning of the word *microcosm.* Then write two sentences, each describing a different kind of microcosm.

List 2

Write a question about one of the words in List 2, showing that you understand its meaning. An example question for the word *geology* is: *Which word describes the study of the composition of Earth?*

List 3

Write one sentence using as many of the list words as you can. Challenge yourself. Can you use all four words in one sentence?

Rap It Up Working with a classmate, choose a word from the week's lesson. Use the word and its definition to create a short poem or rap. Compile your rap with other classmates' raps into a Rap It Up notebook.

LIST WORDS

area
bisect
congruent
convert
cubic
dimension
mass
perimeter

Use Context as Clues to Meaning

In geometry, a branch of mathematics, the word *area* means "the amount of surface, usually measured in square units." The word comes from the Latin word *area,* which means "a level piece of ground." At the right are more words related to math. You may come across these words in your math class.

Look at the drawings and information below. How does the context help you understand the meanings of the underlined words?

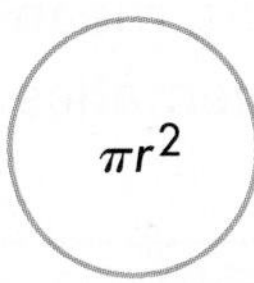

Use this formula to measure the area of the space covered by the circle.

1 kg = 2.2 lb

You can convert, or change, a metric measurement to a standard one.

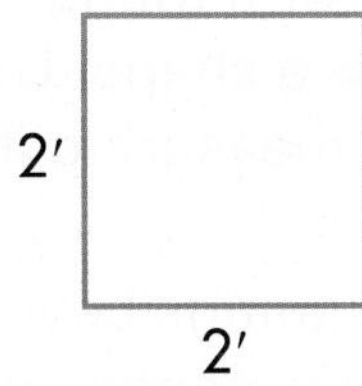

The measurements show the dimensions, or the length and width, of this square.

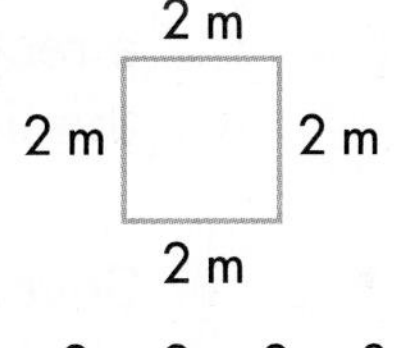

2 + 2 + 2 + 2 = 8 m

Measure the outside perimeter of a shape, or the distance around it.

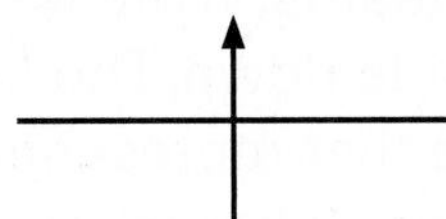

The arrow bisects the line. It cuts it in half.

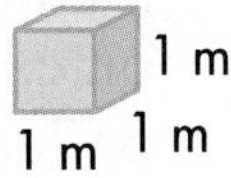

Anything shaped like a cube is cubic.

The sides of both triangles are equal. The triangles are congruent.

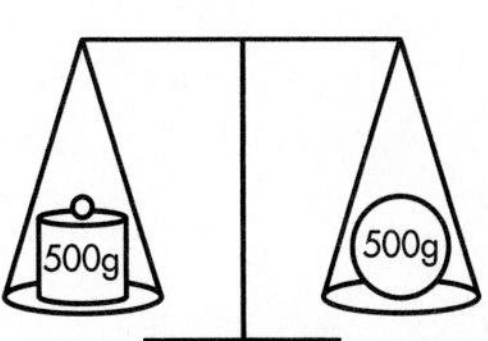

Mass is the quantity of matter in an object.

In Your Notebook Write each list word. Draw a picture for each.

Related Words

Two of the list words—*dimension* and *perimeter*—share the *metria* root, which means "measuring." Other related words you may come across in your math class are *meter, metric, symmetrical,* and *parameter*. Knowing how words are related can help you better understand the meanings of the words.

The list word *convert* has the Latin root *vert,* meaning "turn." Related words you may encounter in mathematics are *converge, converse, vertex,* and *vertical.*

Did you know?

Congruent comes from a Latin word meaning "coming together." It is often used figuratively for things that fit well together. *Incongruous* means the opposite: "out of place" or "inappropriate."

Apply and Extend

- Can you measure a circle's perimeter or a triangle's area? Does a rectangle have dimensions? Choose a shape. Use as many of the list words as you can to describe measuring it.
- Several words in this lesson have meanings beyond those in mathematics. Choose a word. Write one sentence using its math meaning. Write another sentence demonstrating another meaning.

The Illustrated Word Sharpen your pencils—it's time to play a picture game. Divide a group into two teams. Write lesson words on cards and place them in a stack upside down. The first person on Team 1 takes a card, draws a picture that represents the word on the card, and shows the picture to his or her team. If team members guess the word in 30 seconds, the team gets a point. Now it's Team 2's turn.

claim, clam — LIST 1

acclaim
claimant
clamor
declaim
exclaim
exclamation
reclamation

Claim is a Latin root that means "to shout" or "call out." Another way to spell this root is ***clam***.

- Words containing *claim* or *clam* usually have something to do with calling out or announcing.
- Use *claim* and *clam* as clues to meaning when you come across words that contain this root.

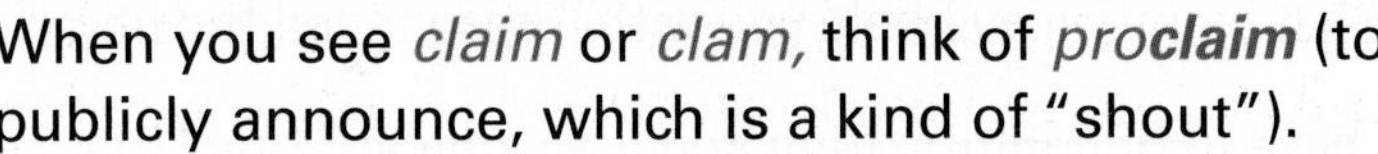

ANCHOR WORD **proclaim**

When you see *claim* or *clam,* think of *pro**claim*** (to publicly announce, which is a kind of "shout").

Clues to Meaning Use *claim* and *clam* as clues to the meanings of the underlined words.

The scene in front of the courthouse was much different from the happy cries of praise and <u>acclaim</u> the politician had once enjoyed. His speech could hardly be heard over the loud shouts and <u>exclamations</u>. The <u>clamor</u> of the crowd was getting louder and louder. An employee had said the politician was a thief. The politician denied the <u>claimant's</u> charges against him and, in a formal speech, tried to <u>declaim</u> that he was innocent. Regardless of what the politician might <u>exclaim</u>, his shouts were not likely to change the public's minds about him. He was more likely to receive a jail sentence than <u>reclamation</u> of his reputation! No, his reputation could not be saved.

ques, quir, quer, quis — LIST 2

inquiry
query
quest
questionable
requisition

Ques is a Latin root that means "ask" or "seek." Other ways to spell this root are ***quir, quer,*** and ***quis***.

- Words containing *ques, quir, quer,* or *quis* usually have something to do with asking a question.

When you see *ques, quir, quer,* or *quis,* think of ***ques**tion* (a statement that "asks" for or "seeks" information).

Clues to Meaning Use *ques, quir, quer,* and *quis* as clues to the meanings of the underlined words.

Ling's teacher assigned each student a quest—a search to find information about any animal. Unsure of how to find the information, Ling approached the librarian. "I have a question," she said.

"What inquiry may I help you with?" responded the librarian.

"I have to find information about an animal," said Ling. "I chose the quetzal, a bird in Costa Rica."

"That might be a questionable, or problematic, choice," she remarked. "Our library doesn't have any material on it. I could query other libraries to ask them and requisition the books to be sent here."

In Your Notebook Write each list word and a clue to its meaning. To check a meaning, use a dictionary.

Dictionary Pronunciations

Use the dictionary to help with pronunciations. For example, look up the word *exclamation*. Following the entry word is the pronunciation (ek′ sklə mā′ shən).

The accent marks (′ ′) indicate which syllables to emphasize when you speak. The main accent is shown by the primary mark (′). Emphasize this syllable more than the others. The symbol (′) is the secondary mark. In the word *exclamation*, the third syllable has a primary accent (′) and the first has a secondary accent (′).

The symbol ə is the schwa, pronounced (shwä). It is an unstressed vowel sound, such as the *a* in *about* and the *e* in *taken*. In the word *exclamation*, the second and fourth syllables each contain a schwa.

Apply and Extend

List 1

Write a question about one of the list words that contains *claim* or *clam*, showing that you understand the meaning of the word. An example of a question for the word *clamor* is *"Which word describes a loud and continued outcry or noise?"*

List 2

The word *proclaim* means "to announce or declare in an official manner." Think about how *acclaim, declaim, exclaim,* and *proclaim* are related in meaning. Write one or two sentences using at least three of the four words.

List 2

The list words *query* and *requisition* can be used as nouns or verbs. Look up the multiple meanings of both words. For each one, write a sentence using a noun form and a sentence using a verb form. Include context to show you understand the meanings of the words.

Clue Review Play this word game with one of your classmates. Choose one of the list words. Give your partner a clue about the word. Did your partner guess the word correctly? If not, provide another clue until your partner correctly identifies the word. Then switch roles.

Did you know?

Remember, *ques* is a Latin root that means "to ask" or "to seek." In Latin texts, the word *quaestio* was written at the beginning of a sentence that asked a question. The modern question mark didn't come into use until the middle of the nineteenth century.

LIST WORDS

anxiously
bellow
curtly
indignantly
plead
smirk
smugly
sputter

Use Context as Clues to Meaning

Interesting conversation between characters can make all the difference in a story. When authors use precise words, rather than simply "he said/she said," the writing becomes much more exciting.

Read these sentences.

> The boy said, "I found it."
> The boy **nervously mumbled**, "I found it."
> The boy **happily exclaimed**, "I found it."

Say "I found it" as described in the last two sentences.

The word *exclaim* has the Latin root *claim,* which means "shout" or "cry out." Knowing the meaning of *claim* helps you know how the boy speaks. Why would an author use *exclaim* rather than *said?*

Read this lunchroom conversation. How does the context help you understand the meanings of the underlined words?

- Judith was so nervous about an upcoming test that she accidentally knocked over Grey's juice and anxiously sputtered, saying over and over, "I am sorry, sorry, so sorry."
- Omar didn't make an effort to be polite, and would often just comment abruptly on whether he liked a particular dish. So, it was no surprise when he curtly said, "Same old burned sausages."
- Grace just grinned a self-satisfied grin and smirked, "Chill, my friend. Too rude, no food. You need to take a breath."
- When Billy threw a napkin at Hazel, she gave him a displeasing look and said indignantly, "Why don't you just grow up, Billy?"
- Blake was sure that he got the better deal when he traded lunches with Porter and smugly remarked, "Enjoy your lunch, Porter!"
- Although Porter was not in the habit of begging, he had indeed pleaded with Blake to trade lunches. But now that he saw the contents of Blake's lunch bag, he was furious and bellowed loudly, "Blake, this is not what you said you had for lunch. You said you had a *ham,* not a *clam,* sandwich. I hate clams."

In Your Notebook Write each list word and its meaning. Then write the words or phrases from the context sentences that helped you figure out the meaning of each word.

Did you know?

Anxious comes from a Latin word meaning "to choke." Fear can cause a choking feeling. If you are too anxious to do well in a game, and you do the opposite, and you don't do well at all, then some may say you *choked*.

Using an Online Thesaurus

An online thesaurus is a digital book of synonyms, or words that share similar meanings. For example, *tense, apprehensive, uneasy, concerned,* and *perturbed* are all synonyms of the word *anxious*. Not every word has a synonym. Some words, such as *uncle,* do not have synonyms and are not included in a thesaurus.

For an online thesaurus, type in the word and click "enter" or "search." A list of synonyms for your word will appear.

- Read through the words that the thesaurus lists as synonyms.
- Choose the word that best expresses your intended meaning.
- Check a dictionary to make sure you are using the synonym correctly.

Apply and Extend

- Think about a conversation you have had at school. Write what someone said to you in that conversation. Use list words to describe how the person spoke.
- Choose one of the list words. Use a thesaurus to find synonyms for that word. Write a sentence using the list word and another sentence using one of its synonyms.

Act It Out Put your acting talent to work. Work with several classmates to perform a skit based on the passages in this lesson. Choose a narrator and students to play the characters in the passage. Become your character!

LIST 1

advocate
equivocal
vocalist
vocation
vociferous

voc

Voc is a Latin root that means "call."

- Words containing *voc* usually have something to do with calling.
- Use *voc* as a clue to meaning when you come across words that contain this root.

When you see *voc,* think of ***voc**al* (to "call" with your voice).

Clues to Meaning Use *voc* as a clue to the meanings of the underlined words.

- The vocalist trained his voice for years before becoming the lead singer for the Rockfish. When asked in an interview if he was interested in leaving the group to pursue a solo career, he gave an equivocal answer, which was confusing. He said, "Maybe I would, and then again maybe I wouldn't."
- A noisy, vociferous crowd shouted at the lawyer and her client as they left the courthouse. The crowd was unhappy with the "not guilty" verdict, but the lawyer believed that her client was innocent. Madeline took pride in her vocation as an attorney because sometimes she could help people who had been wrongly accused. An advocate of justice for all, she frequently spoke in favor of a fairer legal system.

age, ade

LIST 2

blockade
escapade
marriage
pilgrimage
promenade
rummage
voyage

Age is a Latin suffix that means "action" or "process." Another way to spell this suffix is ***ade***.

- To figure out words with the suffix *age* or *ade,* identify the root or base word first and then add the meaning "action of" or "process of."

When you see *age* or *ade,* think of *leak**age*** (the "process" of leaking).

Clues to Meaning Use *age* and *ade* as clues to the meanings of the underlined words.

Christa Ryan and I have a funny story about our marriage. We wanted to have a wild adventure, an escapade that we could remember for the rest of our lives.

Ryan We decided to run to South America to become husband and wife. We sneaked aboard a ship, and our voyage began.

Christa At sea, the captain announced that enemy ships had set up a blockade at the next port. Because we couldn't enter that port, we had to keep sailing.

Ryan At night, we would promenade around the ship's deck until we were too tired to walk anymore.

Christa We had to rummage for food by hunting for scraps in the dining room as diners left.

Ryan During the day, we hid in the cargo section and talked about how we would someday tell our children about our pilgrimage to get married. This journey would always be a very special one for us.

In Your Notebook Write each list word and its meaning. Look for the context clues in the passage to help you find the meanings.

Mythological Allusions

Writers often include references to Greek and Roman myths in their stories or essays. These references are called mythological allusions. You learned that the word *marriage* means "the act of living together as husband and wife." If a writer wanted to tell a story about a secret marriage between two people from warring countries, he or she might make a reference to Cupid, the Roman god of love. Cupid carried a bow and arrow, and anyone shot with one of his arrows fell in love.

Have you heard these expressions?

- bon voyage
- a maiden voyage
- a marriage made in heaven

Apply and Extend

List 1

Choose two words from the list and write an imaginative book title for each one. The titles should reflect the meaning of the words.

List 2

The words in this list have the suffix *age* or *ade*. Choose a list word and use it in a sentence. Then, write two more words that have the suffix and explain their meanings. Search suffix lists online if you have difficulty figuring out words on your own.

List 2

Choose a word and write a sentence that connects that word to some kind of adventure. For example: *If you take a pilgrimage to a shrine, you may run into an unexpected adventure on the journey.*

Rap It Up Working with a classmate, choose words from the week's lesson. Use the words and their definitions to create a short poem or rap. Compile your rap with other classmates' raps into a Rap It Up notebook.

Use Context as Clues to Meaning

Writers and prose go together like peanut butter and jelly. The word *prose* comes from a Latin word *prosa,* meaning "straight speech," and is used in the world of reading and writing. At the right are more words related to spoken and written language. You may come across these words in your language arts class.

Read about ways writers use language. How does the context help you understand the meanings of the underlined words?

When you read a novel, a play, or an article, you are reading prose. Sometimes an editor will revise a writer's prose to make it clearer. For instance, sometimes writers use words or expressions that should be replaced to make the writing better. One example is an archaism, a word or expression from long ago that is no longer used—such as using *ere* for *before*. Another example is a euphemism, a word or phrase used in place of unpleasant language to avoid offending a reader. For example, a writer might say someone is "indisposed" instead of "in the bathroom." Doublespeak, which is related to euphemisms, is indirect or complex language used to trick or mislead a reader, such as advertising cars as "pre-owned" instead of "used."

Writers often use figures of speech to make their writing more interesting. They can use similes to compare two unlike things using the words *like* or *as,* or metaphors to compare two unlike things without using *like* or *as*. Symbolism, or the use of something to suggest a different meaning, is another way writers can add interest and complexity to their work. For example, a heart is commonly used as a symbol for love. While figures of speech can make writing more lively, clichés, which are overused expressions, can make writing dull. "White as snow" and "good as gold" are clichés.

LIST WORDS

archaism
cliché
doublespeak
euphemism
metaphor
prose
simile
symbolism

In Your Notebook Write each list word and add an example that shows your understanding of the word.

Using an Online Dictionary

If you are unclear about the meaning of a word, such as *euphemism,* you can look up its definition in an online dictionary.

- Enter the word into the dictionary's search engine and hit "Enter" or "Return."
- Read through the definition and examples to make sure you understand the word and how it's used in context.
- Note that online dictionary entries usually provide the word's part of speech, origins, and an audio pronunciation.

An online dictionary can be a helpful tool for you to quickly look up words as you read and write.

Did you know?
In one of his plays, William Shakespeare wrote the metaphor "All the world's a stage."

Apply and Extend

- Similes and metaphors express comparisons of two unlike things. Write a sentence for each type of comparison that includes an example.

- When writers use symbolism, they include a symbol to stand for something beyond its usual meaning. For example, an olive branch is a common symbol for peace. Write a sentence or two to explain another common symbol.

Skit Work with a team. Choose a word from the word list and create a skit with examples to illustrate its meaning. For example, you could do a humorous skit with examples of clichés.

terre, terra, terri LIST 1

subterranean
terrace
terra cotta
terrain
terrarium
territory

Terre is a Latin root that means "earth." Other ways to spell this root are ***terra*** and ***terri.***

- Words containing *terre, terra,* or *terri* usually have something to do with land or the Earth.
- Use *terre, terra,* and *terri* as clues to meaning when you come across words that contain this root.
- The word *extraterrestrial* has a Latin prefix and a Latin root.

extra (outside) + terre (earth) = extraterrestrial

When you see *terre, terra,* or *terri,* think of *extra**terre**strial* (something that is outside the "Earth").

Clues to Meaning Use *terre, terra,* and *terri* as clues to the meanings of the underlined words.

Looking out at the brick patio behind their house, the twins talked about the beauty of their terrace and how they would miss it when they left. The area was full of terra cotta pots, brownish-red earthenware their mother made when they were young. A large terrarium filled with exotic plants stood next to the gate. They passed it as they boarded their spaceship. They were going to the Subterranean Territory, an underground land where the caverns were so deep that it took days to descend to the bottom. The twins were excited one moment and scared the next. That area was new terrain for them, with dark, rocky passageways and the occasional dragon.

LESSON 35

LIST 2 ary, ory, ery

confectionery
conservatory
dormitory
infirmary
laboratory
sanctuary

Ary is a Latin suffix that means "place for." Other ways to spell this suffix are ***ory*** and ***ery***.

- Words containing *ary, ory,* or *ery* usually have something to do with locations.
- The word *library* has a Latin root and a Latin suffix.

liber (book) + ary (place for) = library

When you see *ary, ory,* or *ery,* think of *library* (a "place for" books).

Clues to Meaning Use *ary, ory,* and *ery* as clues to the meanings of the underlined words.

Winston Are you on your way to the laboratory to work on that science project?

Lesley No, I just left my job at the confectionery. I think I ate too many sweets. I'm headed for the infirmary. I'm not feeling well.

Winston What a great place to work! Candy whenever you want it! All I do is water plants at the conservatory.

Lesley The conservatory must be peaceful. I used to work at a sanctuary where wildlife lived unharmed. Meet me later at my dormitory where I'm living now that I'm in college, and I'll show you pictures of the different wildlife protected at the sanctuary.

In Your Notebook Write the list words. Then, draw a city plan or map and try to include as many of the places from List 2 as possible. Label the places and draw symbols or pictures that represent the meaning of the word.

Word Roots

Place-names are often not translated from one language into another, so you will frequently encounter place-names in other languages. For example, at latitude 54° South and longitude 69° West, you will find Tierra del Fuego at the southern tip of South America. Even if you don't speak Portuguese, you may recognize the connection of *Tierra* to the English words *territory* and *terrestrial* through the Latin root *terra* (earth). *Fuego* (fire) comes from the Latin word *focus,* which means "hearth."

Apply and Extend

List 1

Though they sound like they might share a root, *terrible* and *territory* have different origins. Explain in a sentence or two how the etymologies of these words differ. Consult a dictionary for help.

List 1

Use the words from the list to tell a brief story about the Earth.

List 2

If you sleep in a *dormitory* and raise plants in a *conservatory,* what would you do in an *observatory?* All of the words from this list are a location, or a place. Tell how the words *glossary* and *dictionary* are also places, and explain what they are places for.

Did you know?
The Mediterranean Sea is so named because the ancient civilizations that lived around its shores believed it was "the sea in the middle of the Earth." Which list word can you find in the word *Mediterranean*?

Act It Out Literature is rich with adventure stories set deep under the Earth's surface. One of the most famous works in this genre is Jules Verne's *A Journey to the Center of the Earth.* Put your acting talent to work. Think about what it might be like to travel or live underground. With several classmates, discuss ideas about living a subterranean life. Choose a narrator and students to play characters in a short scene. Use as many list words in the scene as you can.

LESSON 36 Domain-Specific Vocabulary

Science

LIST WORDS

battery
circuit
electricity
magnet
property
residue
sample
systematic

Use Context as Clues to Meaning

The word *electricity* has a surprising origin. It comes from the Greek root *elektron*, which means "amber." While the ancient Greeks did not know as much about electricity as we do, they did understand that rubbing a substance such as amber produces a tiny charge that attracts other materials or even creates a small spark. Scientists in the 1600s created the word *electricity* to mean "like amber in the way it attracts."

Today, almost every place you go uses electricity. The library uses it to provide lighting, and if you use a computer there, it too runs on electricity. Students who live in a dormitory use electric lights and computers, as well as refrigerators, microwave ovens, and televisions. At the left are words related to electricity and general science. You may come across these words in your science class.

Read these sentences. How does the context help you figure out the meanings of the underlined words?

- Scientific work in the laboratory must be carried out in a systematic and orderly way.
- Before construction can begin, soil experts must sample, or test, a small section of the terrain for toxins.
- The main power source for the experiment is a battery.
- Unfortunately, the cleaning solution may leave behind a white residue.
- Lodestone is a mineral that was once thought to have magic powers. Its unique properties, or qualities, make it function like a magnet because it has the power to attract iron and steel.
- The lightning storm caused a surge of electrical current to blow the circuit and cut the electricity to an entire neighborhood, which made the lights go out.

In Your Notebook Write the list words and the scientific definition of each. Add a sketch to a definition, if appropriate.

Multiple Meanings

Some of the list words in this lesson have both specific scientific meanings and more general ones. For instance, *property* can be something you own or a piece of land. Or, if used in a scientific sense, *property* can describe a quality or power belonging to something, as in the *healing property of sleep*.

When you come upon an unknown word in your reading, first try to figure out the meaning based on context clues in the surrounding text. How is the word used in the text you are reading? Then, to confirm your understanding, consult a dictionary. Be sure to read through all of the definitions given for a word to find the one that fits what you are reading.

Did you know?

Don't confuse *systematic* with *systemic*. The first means having a plan or being orderly; the second describes something having to do with a system, often within the body—a *systemic* disease.

Apply and Extend

- The word *battery* has several different meanings, all of which come from the same root. Use a dictionary or go online to discover how these meanings are related to that root and write a sentence of explanation.
- Choose two of the list words. Write a sentence for each, expressing its general meaning as opposed to its scientific meaning.

Word History Choose an interesting word from this week's lesson. What can you find out about the history and origins of your word? Answer the following questions:

- From which language did your word derive?
- What is the first recorded instance of its use in the English language?
- What is one interesting fact you learned about the word?
- List related words that you find.

LESSON 37 Word Parts and Meanings

term, ten

LIST 1

determine
exterminate
interminable
predetermine
term
terminate

term

Term is a Latin root that means "end."

- Words containing *term* usually have something to do with an end or boundary. *Term* is also a word that has many definitions, one of which is "a set period of time." The terms of an agreement are its boundaries or limits. If you agree to do something until the end of a certain day, then on the day after that, the agreement has come to an end and is no longer valid.
- Use *term* as a clue to meaning when you come across words that contain this root.

When you see *term,* think of ***terminal*** (final or having to do with the "end" of something).

Clues to Meaning Use *term* as a clue to the meanings of the underlined words.

- To determine, or figure out, who stole the diamonds, the police looked at fingerprints left around the box where the diamonds had been stored.
- Medical researchers and doctors hope to exterminate the polio virus worldwide. If the virus is completely destroyed, no one will get polio.
- The wait for dinner seemed interminable. We wondered if it would ever be ready.
- I want to predetermine how much money we can spend on the school field trip next week. If I am able to do this in advance, we can start planning how we will spend the money.
- Every U.S. President is elected to a term of four years. Near the end of that period of time, he or she can run for reelection to one more term.
- Saturday will be my last day of work. That's when this job will end and our agreement will terminate.

ten

LIST 2

- extension
- intensity
- tendency
- tendon
- tendril
- tension

Ten is a Latin root that means "stretch."

- The word *extend* has two Latin roots.

  ex (out) + tend (stretch) = extend (to stretch out)

When you see *ten,* think of *extension cord* (something that "stretches" an appliance's cord).

Clues to Meaning Use *ten* as a clue to the meanings of the underlined words.

- Patrick asked for an <u>extension</u> of the deadline for his article. He needed extra time to research his topic.
- Jorge plays tennis with great <u>intensity</u>. He puts all his energy into staying focused and working hard.
- Li has a <u>tendency</u> to be happy. It seems she's that way naturally.
- Sometimes doctors must repair <u>tendons</u>, the tissues that connect muscles to bones or other body parts, if the <u>tendons</u> are badly injured.
- The <u>tendrils</u> of the ivy climbed up the side of Grandma's house. The thin branches attached themselves to the bricks.
- The <u>tension</u> increased when the werewolf walked in. People started to get anxious as they waited to find out what would happen next.

In Your Notebook Write a definition for each list word in your own words.

Multiple Meanings

Notice how *extension* is used in two different ways in this sentence.

I baked cookies for my boss as an <u>extension</u> of my gratitude for getting my own phone <u>extension</u> at work, which allowed customers to call me through our switchboard.

Context clues, such as examples and explanations, can help you determine the meaning of each use of the word *extension*. For example, "I baked cookies" is an example of an extension of gratitude. Based on this context, you can infer that *extension* means "act of reaching out."

Apply and Extend

List 1

Look up the word *terminal* and write all of the meanings you find for it as a noun. How does each meaning connect to the root *term?*

List 1

What do *interminable* and *terminate* mean? Explain why these words are antonyms.

List 2

This list contains the words *tendon* and *tendril*. How are they related in meaning? Write a sentence for each, using context to show you understand their meanings.

Clue Review Play a word game with one of your classmates. Choose one of the list words. Give your partner a clue about the word. Did your partner guess the word correctly? If not, provide another clue until your partner correctly identifies the word. Then switch roles.

LIST WORDS

ancestor
emigrate
immigrate
migration
mission
pilgrim
predecessor
refugee

Use Context as Clues to Meaning

When did your family come to the United States? Perhaps your great-grandparents came here by boat from another country years ago. Or maybe your parents arrived at a local airport. You and your family may even have arrived here recently. Your family members who were born before you are your *forebears*.

At the right are words that might be used to tell the stories of our forebears. You may come across these words in your social studies class.

Read about how people first came to the United States. How does the context help you understand the meanings of the underlined words?

Most people living in the United States are here because their ancestors emigrated from another country. This may have happened long ago, when a great-great-grandparent moved here; thirty or forty years ago when a grandparent came here; or even more recently, when a parent traveled here. People have had different reasons for immigrating, or settling, in the United States.

In the 1600s and 1700s, travelers arriving on the east coast of the "New World" may have been pilgrims coming from England seeking religious freedom. Two hundred years later, a traveler arriving at Ellis Island in New York Harbor might have been a refugee escaping starvation or political or ethnic persecution in his or her country. Many were looking for jobs.

In the 1700s, a person from Spain might have traveled to what would become California to set up a mission. Missions were established by religious orders to provide food and shelter to travelers but also to convert local Native Americans to Catholicism.

As you see, migration from one country to another is quite common among all people at all times. The stories of how our ancestors came to the United States can be very interesting. Do you know any stories about how predecessors in your community, or people who came before you, decided to settle there?

In Your Notebook Write each list word and its meaning. Include a word or phrase from the reading that helped you understand the list word.

Context Clues

If you come across a word you don't know, you can often use the surrounding text to infer the word's meaning. Common context clues are synonyms, antonyms, explanations, and examples. For example, if a text includes *great-grandparent* as an example of an *ancestor*, it can help you determine that an *ancestor* is a person from whom you are descended.

Read the following text for two different clues to the meaning of *peripatetic.*

Some Native Americans led a peripatetic *existence, wandering from one place to another in response to seasonal changes or to find food. A nomadic lifestyle had certain advantages: it meant fresh game, fresh pasture, and opportunities for friendship and trade with people outside their community.*

Can you figure out the meaning of *peripatetic?* The text includes an explanation ("wandering from one place to another") and a synonym (*nomadic*).

Did you know?

You may hear the French word *émigré* in English as often as the English equivalent *emigrant*. Some of the first *émigrés* in the United States came from France during the French Revolution.

Apply and Extend

- Which two words in the list are synonyms? Write a sentence or two using the words that demonstrates the shades of differences in their meanings.
- Which two words in the list are antonyms? What prefixes are used to give the words opposite meanings? Write a sentence using both words.

Graphic Gallery Use your skills as an artist to create a mini graphic novel on the topic of forebears, using words from this week's lesson. Draw pictures and write dialogue or use an online program to create the graphic text. How many of the words can you use? Compile the class's illustrated stories into a Graphic Gallery.

vol, volv

LIST 1

convoluted
devolve
evolution
involvement
revolve
volume

Vol is a Latin root that means "roll" or "turn." Another way to spell this root is ***volv***.

- Words containing *vol* or *volv* usually have to do with something rolling or turning.
- Use *vol* and *volv* as clues to meaning when you come across words that contain this root.

When you see *vol* or *volv,* think of *re**vol**ution* (one "turn" around a central point).

Clues to Meaning Use *vol* and *volv* as clues to the meanings of the underlined words.

Carla I finished the last book in the vampire series, but the author could have written the story in one <u>volume</u> rather than three.

Jan From what I heard, the story was about the <u>evolution</u> of two characters as they aged. It seems to have taken the author a long time to explain how they grew and changed over the years.

Carla Yes, the plot <u>revolves</u>, or circles, around two vampires. They do change, but their <u>involvement</u> in so many activities made the plot very hard to follow. I just couldn't keep track of all the different things they participated in. I've never read a more <u>convoluted</u> and complicated story in my life! I think the author got confused too! At the end, she let the plot <u>devolve</u> and deteriorate into a bunch of meaningless nonsense. I wouldn't recommend this series to anyone!

Did you know?
In Roman times, the word *volume* referred to books written on "rolls" of parchment.

LIST 2 grad

degradation
downgrade
gradation
gradient
gradual
undergraduate

Grad is a Latin root that means "step."

- Words containing *grad* usually have something to do with changing by steps or degrees.

When you see *grad,* think of ***grade*** (a "step" in elementary or high school).

Clues to Meaning Use *grad* as a clue to the meanings of the underlined words.

- In high school, moving from freshman year to senior year in steps is an example of gradation.
- Students at universities and colleges who have not yet completed the steps to graduation are called undergraduates.
- Don't downgrade, or minimize, the importance of this assignment.
- The gradient of a surface is its slope. Some skateboarders challenge themselves by skating on a road with a steep gradient.
- Though the changes were gradual, little by little his health was improving.
- Erosion has caused the degradation of many cliffs. The rock formations are wearing away due to a combination of wind, water, and waves.

In Your Notebook Write each list word and its meaning in your notebook. Check the meanings in a dictionary. Then choose two words and make a 4-square concept map for each word.

Connotation and Denotation

A word's denotation is its literal meaning. A word's connotation is its suggested meaning beyond a strict dictionary definition. Connotations can be positive, negative, or neutral. For example, the words *convoluted* and *complicated* have similar denotations; both words mean "hard to understand." *Convoluted,* however, has a more negative connotation than *complicated* does, suggesting that something is overly confusing or intricate. As you read and write, be aware that many words can imply a range of meanings. This will help you understand what you read and help you select the best words for your intended purpose as you write.

Apply and Extend

List 1

Write one sentence using as many of the list words as you can. Challenge yourself.

List 1

Work with a partner to choose a word and write a "What if" question. For example, *What if a speaker gave a convoluted explanation about a scientific concept?* An answer to this question might be *The audience might be confused by the convoluted explanation.*

List 2

Think about how *gradation, gradient,* and *gradual* are related in meaning. What is the gradation of a gradual gradient? Write a sentence or two using these three words.

Word Part Invention How much of a wordsmith are you? With a partner, combine word parts from this lesson with other letters or syllables to invent a new word. Then write a definition for the word based on the meanings of the word parts. Share the word and its definition with your classmates.

Did you know?

Evolution comes from the Latin words meaning "to roll" and "out." The English word was originally used about movements of soldiers marching or riding horses, as they separated from one another and spread out over the land.

LIST WORDS

equivalent
fraction
histogram
inequality
linear
proportional
quantitative
quartile

Use Context as Clues to Meaning

On a warm day, you may feel that there has been a gradual increase in temperature. Using your knowledge of math, you can find an exact, or quantitative, measurement of that increase. The word *quantitative* is based on the Latin word *quantus*, meaning "how much." You may come across *quantitative* and the other words in this lesson in your math class.

Read the following explanations of the two illustrations. How do the context and the illustrations help you understand the meanings of the underlined words?

Here's a quantitative description using a linear drawing—a line segment. If you divide the line segment below in half, each part is a fraction, one-half, of the length of the original line segment, so the two parts are equivalent, or equal, to each other in length. Now, if you divide each of the two halves (segments) into two equal parts, the line segment is then divided into four equivalent parts. Segments *AB* and *CD* are proportional to each other (with a 1:1 ratio); they are the same length. However, there is an inequality between segments *AC* and *DE*, because those two segments do not have equal lengths: segment *AC* is longer than, greater than, segment *DE*.

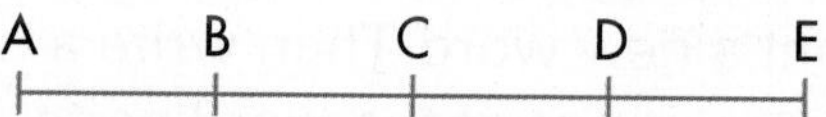

Another way to show quantitative information is with a histogram, or bar graph, like the one below. The graph may be divided into four quartiles, or parts. Each quartile represents 25%, or one-fourth, of the information shown in that bar graph.

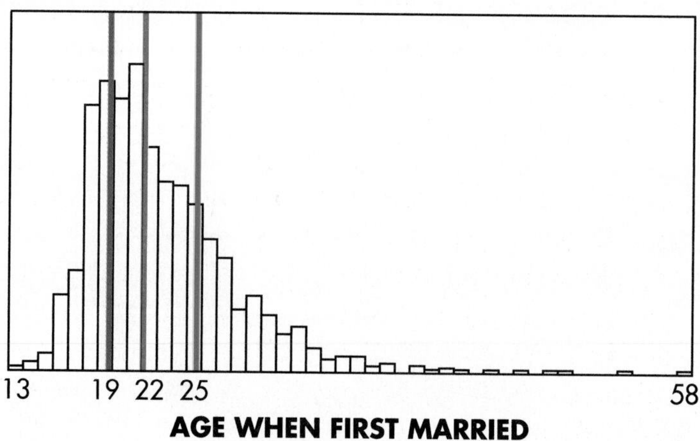

In Your Notebook Write each list word and its meaning. You may want to use an illustration to define the word.

Foreign Words in English

Some ancient Greek and Latin words have become part of our modern English language. The word *quantum* is a form of an ancient Latin word, *quantus*. As you have learned, it means "how much." It is related to *quantitative* and *quantity*, both of which are based on the same Latin word and both of which are used in describing amounts.

The modern, general meaning of *quantum* is "a sum or amount." *Quantum* also has two specialized meanings, both related to physics. It describes a branch of physics that studies how matter and force interact, and it is the name of a basic unit of radiant energy.

Apply and Extend

- *Proportional* refers to a fixed relationship. For example, if your sister is three years younger than you are, your ages will remain proportional as you get older. She will always be three years younger. Write a sentence with an example of things that are mathematically proportional.
- *Equivalent* contains the Latin root *equi*, which means "equal." Find three other words that contain the root *equi*, by either searching online or in a dictionary. Write the words and explain whether their meaning has anything to do with something that is equal.

The Illustrated Word Sharpen your pencils—it's time to play a picture game. Divide a group into two teams. Write lesson words on cards and place them in a stack upside down. The first person on Team 1 takes a card, draws a picture that represents the word on the card, and shows the picture to his or her team. If team members guess the word in 30 seconds, the team gets a point. Now it's Team 2's turn.

Word Parts and Meanings

civ, pub, popul

LIST 1

civics
civil
civility
civilization

civ

Civ is a Latin root that means "citizen."

- Words containing *civ* usually have something to do with citizenship.
- Use *civ* as a clue to meaning when you come across words that contain this root.

When you see *civ,* think of ***civilian*** ("citizen" who is not in the armed forces).

Clues to Meaning Use *civ* as a clue to the meanings of the underlined words.

- As an American citizen, you have <u>civil</u> responsibilities to your local, state, and federal governments. You also have a right to express your opinions freely, but should do so with <u>civility</u> because rude remarks seldom resolve issues. The duties, rights, and privileges of citizens are sometimes studied in <u>civics</u> classes.
- The ancient <u>civilization</u> of Rome prospered as the empire grew. It was an advanced society that made important contributions in art, engineering, and architecture.

LIST 2

popular
popularity
population
populous
publication
publicize
publish
republic

pub, popul

Pub is a Latin root that means "people." Another way to spell this root is ***popul.***

- The word *popular* comes from the Latin *populous,* which means "people."

When you see *pub* or *popul,* think of ***public*** ("people" in general).

Clues to Meaning Use *pub* and *popul* as clues to the meanings of the underlined words.

Augustus, the first Roman emperor, convinced the citizens he had restored the earlier republic and would give them more voice in electing representatives. ~~Liked and~~ admired by the people, Augustus kept control because of his popularity. At the time of his rule, Rome was populous, with many people per square mile; the population probably numbered more than a million people. Chariot races and gladiator fights drew large crowds and were popular forms of entertainment.

Augustus encouraged and supported the arts, including literature. The publication, or production, of reading materials in ancient Rome relied on the copying of works by hand on scrolls. To publish, or offer their works to the people, writers went to book dealers because they also employed the copiers. To publicize, or announce their new works to the public, writers gave readings.

In Your Notebook Write each list word. Next to it, write the root. Explain briefly how the meaning of the root relates to the word.

Analogy Study

One kind of analogy is a comparison between two pairs of words that are related in some way. Among the relationships shown in analogies are words with similar meanings. For example: civility is to courtesy as popular is to liked. Here is an analogy with opposites: civil is to rude as publicize is to conceal. The words in each pair are antonyms. Analogies can also be written as shown below.

civility is to courtesy as popular is to liked

civil : rude :: publicize : conceal

Apply and Extend

List 1

Write one sentence using as many of the list words as you can. Challenge yourself. Can you use all four words in one sentence?

List 2

How are *publication, publicize,* and *publish* related? Would you *publicize* or *publish* a publication? Or, could you do both? Which would you need to do first? Write a sentence or two using these three words.

List 2

Choose two of the following terms and use each one in a sentence that explains its meaning: *public enemy, public opinion, public school, public service, public speaking, public works.*

Did you know?

- *Civil servants* are employed in government service.
- *Civil war* is a war between opposing groups within a nation.

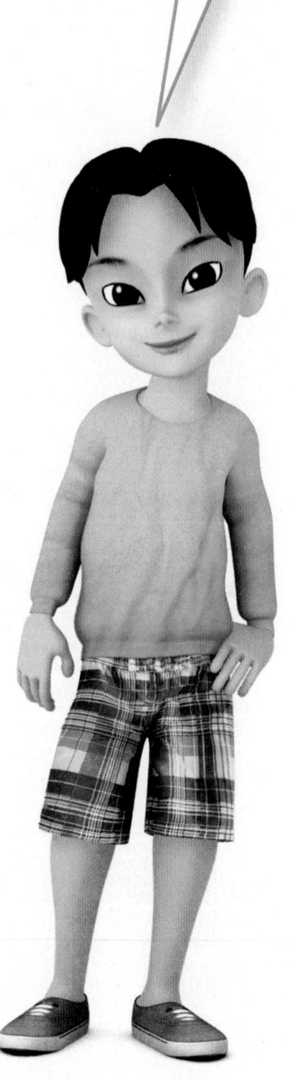

Clue Review Play a word game with one of your classmates. Choose one of the list words. Give your partner a clue about the word. You can act out the word, if you need to. Did your partner guess the word correctly? If not, provide another clue until your partner correctly identifies the word. Then switch roles.

LIST WORDS

aphorism
authenticity
candidly
deception
falsehood
plausible
validity
veracity

Use Context as Clues to Meaning

Throughout history, various civilizations have valued what is true, honest, and factual. Some well-known sayings about truth include the following.

- "If you tell the *truth*, you don't have to remember anything." —Mark Twain
- "The high-minded man must care more for truth than what people think." —Aristotle

Read this reporter's interview with a candidate for city council. How does the context help you understand the meanings of the underlined words?

Interviewer You have accused the current city council of accepting bribes. Candidly, what do you really know about this? Please be honest.

Candidate I know that my story seems unlikely, but remember the aphorism, "Truth is stranger than fiction." There's practical wisdom and truth in that saying.

Interviewer Let's get back to your accusation. How can the public believe its validity, or know whether or not it's legally sound? Do you have facts that support your charges?

Candidate One council member admitted the deception, or trickery, to me. What happened was that the city council chose a company to do some work because the company gave money to some council members. That company was charging the most money for the work, so the taxpayers were definitely cheated.

Interviewer Is the council member's account credible? Are you able to prove whether or not it's true—its veracity?

Candidate The details the council member provided seem plausible and believable, and I do think his claims are true.

Interviewer Won't it be difficult to prove authenticity, or reliability, based on the word of just one person?

Candidate I stand by my accusation. Several disloyal council members have told falsehoods. They should be voted off the council for telling those lies.

In Your Notebook Write each list word. Next to each word, except *aphorism,* write a plus sign (+) to mean that the word represents something true, or a minus sign (–) to mean that the word represents something false.

Word Story

Hippocrates first used the word *aphorism* to describe short truths, often of a medical nature. Probably his most famous aphorism is "Life is short, art long, opportunity fleeting, experience misleading, judgment difficult." Eventually aphorisms were applied to other fields, such as physical science and law. Now they are considered to be short and clever sayings that convey a general truth. Here are a few examples of aphorisms:

"Hindsight is 20/20."

"Love all, trust a few, do wrong to none." —William Shakespeare

"Lost time is never found again." —Benjamin Franklin

Apply and Extend

- Do an online search for a quote about truth or falsehood. Write down your quote and its source. Explain what your quote means to you.

- Write a sentence that includes one of the list words. Show that you understand the word's meaning by providing a synonym that helps define the word in context.

Act It Out Put your acting talent to work. Work with several classmates to perform a skit based on the reporter's interview with a candidate for the city council in this lesson. Choose students to play the characters in the interview. Become your character!

cracy, crat

LIST 1

aristocracy
autocratic
bureaucrat
plutocrat
technocrat
theocracy

Cracy is a Greek root that means "rule." Another spelling for this root is ***crat***.

- Words containing *cracy* or *crat* usually have something to do with government or ruling.
- The word *democracy* has two Greek roots.
  demo (people) + cracy (rule) = democracy

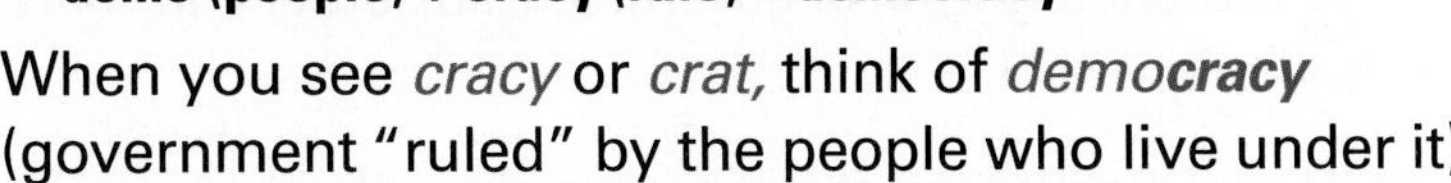

ANCHOR WORD democ**racy**

When you see *cracy* or *crat,* think of *demo**cracy*** (government "ruled" by the people who live under it).

Clues to Meaning Use *cracy* and *crat* as clues to the meanings of the underlined words.

- When the *Titanic* sank in 1912, well-known members of America's wealthy aristocracy, or ruling class, went down with the ship.
- Perhaps only a few people actually want to be a bureaucrat, a government worker who insists on proper paperwork and procedures at the expense of people's needs.
- Former Philippine president Ferdinand Marcos was an autocratic leader, heading a corrupt government and not allowing anyone to disagree with him.
- In ancient Carthage, plutocrats, who governed because they were wealthy, had little regard for citizens that didn't have money.
- A technocrat is a person who favors a government run by people who know how to take advantage of the latest advances in technology.
- In a theocracy, God is recognized as the supreme leader.

archy, arch

LIST 2

anarchist
anarchy
architect
hierarchy
monarch
oligarchy

Archy is a Greek root that means "ruler." Another way to spell this root is ***arch***.

- Words containing *archy* or *arch* usually have something to do with leaders or rulers.
- The word *monarchy* has two Greek roots.
  monos (alone) + archy (rule) = monarchy

When you see *archy* or *arch,* think of *mon**archy*** (governed by one "ruler").

Clues to Meaning Use *archy* and *arch* as clues to the meanings of the underlined words.

- "These anarchists must be stopped!" the duke bellowed, slamming his fist on the table. "If they use violence to overthrow the monarch, we'll be without a king. If we have anarchy, we'll be without any form of government. Disorder and confusion will reign!"
- Manuel disliked the three-person oligarchy that ran the homecoming committee. They should have just let him do it alone, he thought.
- Neva didn't look forward to being a freshman in high school next year. She had enjoyed being at the top of the hierarchy in middle school. The younger students wanted to be like Neva and the other 8th graders. But in high school, she'd be back at the bottom of the new hierarchy. None of the older students would even know or care that she existed!
- I want to be an architect because I have good ideas for new buildings, and I'm also talented at designing them and planning how they should be built.

In Your Notebook Write the list words and one other form of each word. Give the meanings of both the list words and their other forms.

Connotation and Denotation

Words can have literal meaning, or denotation—what you'd find in the dictionary for the word—and a suggested meaning, or connotation. Connotations can be positive or negative.

For example, the denotation of *aristocracy* is "a class of people having a high position in society because of birth, title, or nobility," and its connotation is positive. Synonyms for *aristocracy* include *gentry,* which has a positive connotation, and *upper crust,* which often has a negative connotation.

The denotation of *anarchy* is "the absence of a system of government and law." The word *anarchy* and its synonyms *lawlessness* and *disorder* all have negative connotations.

Did you know?

Bureaucrat includes *bureau,* the French word for "desk." The word *bureaucrat* literally means "desk ruler."

Apply and Extend

List 1

Anarchy, monarchy, oligarchy, and *theocracy* are all forms of government. Write a sentence about two of these forms of government explaining why you think one is better than the other.

List 2

Which form of government in this word list is most likely to have a *hierarchy?* Explain why in a sentence or two.

Rap It Up Working with a classmate, choose a word from the week's lesson. Use the word and its definition to create a short poem or rap about a particular kind of government or leader. Compile your rap with other classmates' raps into a Rap It Up notebook.

LIST WORDS

correlative
declarative
exclamatory
imperative
interrogative
parallelism
participle
rhetoric

Use Context as Clues to Meaning

Many government workers—plutocrats and bureaucrats alike—have learned the value of rhetoric, the art of using words effectively. Its root, *rhetor,* means "orator" or "speaker," and the Greeks used the expression *rhētorikē tekhnē,* meaning "the art of an orator." Today, *rhetoric* also includes the art of writing well. At the left are more words related to writing. You may come across these words in your language arts class.

The word *exclamatory* has the Latin prefix *ex,* the Latin root *clam,* and the Latin suffix *ory.*

ex (out) + clam (to shout) + ory (having to do with) = exclamatory

Writers use exclamatory sentences to add strong emotion to their writing. The sentences below have more things for you to think about as you write. How does the context help you understand the meanings of the underlined words?

- Rhetoric is a fine art. But writing or speaking well is also a craft that requires practice and hard work.
- Use an interrogative sentence when you need to ask a question.
- Use an imperative sentence when you want to make a command or make a request, such as "Please open your book."
- Use a declarative sentence when you have a statement to make.
- Use an exclamatory sentence to convey powerful feelings or strong emotions. (An exclamation mark is usually the correct punctuation for this kind of sentence.)
- Use parallelism, the repetition of a grammatical structure, to communicate your ideas more clearly.
- Correlative conjunctions are used in pairs. For example, *either* and *or* are correlative conjunctions in this sentence: *Either clean your room or walk the dog.*
- A participle is a verb form that can sometimes function as an adjective (for example, "stolen silver").

In Your Notebook Write each list word. What context clues in the sentences help you understand the words? Write the meaning for each word.

Context Clues

Remember that context clues can help you decipher the meanings of words you don't know. One type of context clue to use is an explanation. In the following, see if the words, phrases, and sentences surrounding the underlined word help explain that word.

Rhetoric is a fine art. But writing or speaking well is also a craft that requires practice and hard work.

The phrase "writing or speaking well" explains *rhetoric.* Always look in the text around an unknown word for a clue to its meaning.

Did you know?

The exclamation mark probably comes from the Latin word *io,* which means "a shout of joy." Stacking the I above the O gives you"!".

Apply and Extend

- Choose three words from the word list. For each word, write a sentence that includes context clues for the word. Leave a blank for the word, and ask a classmate to choose the correct word from the word list.
- The words *declarative* and *imperative* describe different kinds of sentences. Write a few sentences to explain the difference between these two kinds of sentences.

Skit With a classmate or two, develop a skit that illustrates the differences among *declarative, imperative, interrogatory,* and *exclamatory* sentences by acting them out.

LESSON 45 Word Parts and Meanings

duct, duc, intro

LIST 1

abduct
conducive
deduce
deduction
educate
productivity
reproduce
viaduct

duct, duc

Duct is a Latin root that means "lead." Another way to spell this root is ***duc***.

- Words containing *duct* or *duc* usually have something to do with leading.
- Use *duct* and *duc* as clues to meaning when you come across words that contain this root.

When you see *duct* or *duc,* think of *con**duct**or* (someone who "leads" an orchestra).

Clues to Meaning Use *duct* and *duc* as clues to the meanings of the underlined words.

The students in another middle school in our city like our mascot, a lemur named Lemmie. They like him so much that they tried to <u>reproduce</u> him, or make a copy of him, out of newspaper and paste. Try as they might, they did not really have the ability to make anything that looked like Lemmie. So basically, their attempts at <u>productivity</u> failed.

Their next move was to <u>abduct</u> Lemmie! Needless to say, kidnapping our mascot was not exactly helpful, or <u>conducive</u>, to creating good school relations. It wasn't hard for us to <u>deduce</u> where they had taken him. We're good at figuring things out and making <u>deductions</u>. Our teachers have <u>educated</u> us in logical thinking. Some of us decided that the thieves had probably hid Lemmie near our school, probably under the <u>viaduct</u> where the train crosses over the highway—and that was exactly where we found him, safe and sound inside his cage.

LIST 2

introduce
introductory
introspective
introvert

intro

Intro is a Latin prefix that means "in" or "within."

- Words beginning with *intro* usually have something to do with leading one in or within.

When you see *intro,* think of ***intro**duction* (something that leads you "in"—to a book, to meeting a person, or to something else).

Clues to Meaning Use *intro* as a clue to the meanings of the underlined words.

- I've never met that teacher. Would you introduce me to her?
- To begin my presentation, I will make introductory remarks about how happy I am to be here.
- She's very quiet and introspective. She sometimes just seems lost in her own thoughts.
- I tend to be an introvert who looks inward for the answers rather than ask someone else for help or advice.

In Your Notebook Write each list word and a clue for each one.

Figurative Language

The list word *introvert* means "a person who thinks rather than acts and does not share private thoughts and emotions with others." The opposite of an introvert is someone who readily displays his or her emotions and has more interest in people and events than in personal thoughts.

People who demonstrate emotion easily can be described as "wearing one's heart on one's sleeve." This expression is an idiom, a type of figurative language that means something other than the literal meaning of the words would indicate.

Other idioms include the following:
the plot thickens: something is becoming complicated
of two minds: indecisive
fish out of water: someone out of place in a new situation

Apply and Extend

List 1

Explain how *deduction, viaduct,* and *abduct* have something to do with "leading."

List 1

Write a question about one of the words, showing that you understand its meaning. An example question for the word *conducive* is: *Which word means "helpful" or "favorable"?*

List 2

Write one sentence using as many of the list words as you can. Challenge yourself. Can you use all four words in one sentence?

Did you know?
Deduction is reasoning from truth to details. Induction is the opposite. It is the process of using details to figure out general truths.

Graphic Gallery Use your skills as a cartoonist to create a comic strip using words from this week's lesson. Draw pictures and write dialogue or use an online program to create the graphic text. How many of the words can you use? Work together with classmates to compile the class's comic strips into a Graphic Gallery.

LIST WORDS

buoyant
centripetal
current
inertia
joule
kinetic
momentum
newton

Use Context as Clues to Meaning

In your science class, you may have conducted experiments to learn about momentum. *Momentum* comes from a Latin word, *movere,* which means "to move." The word describes the motion of a moving body and the force with which the body moves. At the right are more words related to force, energy, and work. You may come across these words in your science class.

Read the following paragraphs about force and motion. How does the context help you understand the meanings of the underlined words?

A centrifuge is a piece of equipment used to separate two substances, one of which is lighter than the other. It uses the principle of centrifugal force, the tendency of an object to move away from the central point around which it is spinning. This is the opposite of centripetal force, the force that tends to move objects *toward* the center around which they are turning.

In a centrifuge, the substances are placed in a container at the end of an arm that spins around a central point. The moving container and the substances in it have kinetic energy, energy caused by motion. At any given moment, they have a particular speed and direction. They also have mass, or quantity of matter. Together, these three characteristics (speed, direction, and mass) determine the container's motion, or momentum.

The spinning causes the heavier substance in the container to move toward the outer part of the container, away from the lighter substance. Why? The answer is inertia. This is the principle that says (1) if objects are moving, they tend to keep doing so with the same speed and direction, and (2) if objects are not moving, they tend to stay at rest. Inertia causes the heavier material to keep traveling in the same direction, making it move away from the center, while the lighter, more buoyant material "floats" *toward* the center.

Force is measured in units called newtons. Another unit of measure is the joule, a unit of energy or work. However, do not confuse energy with electrical current, the flow of electricity through something, such as a wire. Electrical current is often measured in amperes.

In Your Notebook Write the list words. Then choose two words and make a 4-square concept map for each one.

Using a Glossary

Glossaries often accompany texts that have a limited, specific focus. For example, the glossary in this book contains all the lesson words, which include the list words *newton* and *joule* from this lesson. A different book, one about using energy to do work, might have a glossary that contains *newton* and *joule* but also contains the words *ampere* (or *amp*) and *ohm*, which are related to electricity. A glossary is a great help in reading such a text, because it gathers all the words you need in one place for easy reference. A glossary can save you time and eliminate confusion by giving the specific meaning of a term you need to understand in order to read the text. To find the glossary, look in the back of a book for an alphabetical list of terms and their definitions.

Do you know these expressions?

- current events
- gaining momentum
- buoyant personality

Apply and Extend

- There is something interesting about the etymologies of the list words *joule* and *newton*. The words *ampere* and *ohm* also have something unusual about their etymologies. Look up the etymologies of these four words. See if you can discover what they have in common.

- If you talk about *current* in your science class, you are talking about the flow of electricity. However, *current* has other general meanings that you probably know. Use *current* in a sentence that shows its science meaning. Then write two sentences that show general meanings of the word *current*.

Word History Choose an interesting word from this week's lesson. What can you find out about the history and origins of your word? Answer the following questions:

- From which language did your word derive?
- What is the first recorded instance of its use in the English language?
- What is one interesting fact you learned about your word?
- List related words that you find.

mis, mit

LIST 1

demise
emission
intermittent
transmit

Mis is a Latin root that means "to send." Another way to spell this root is ***mit***.

- Words containing *mis* or *mit* usually have something to do with sending something or someone.

ANCHOR WORD **mis**sile

When you see *mis* or *mit,* think of ***mis**sile* (an object "sent" by being thrown or shot).

Clues to Meaning Use *mis* and *mit* as clues to the meanings of the underlined words.

- The car is sending out puffs of black smoke. It must have emission problems! It's an intermittent problem; it happens only now and then.
- The leader had to transmit a radio message to his team telling them that their project had lost its funding. This meant the demise, or end, of the program.

ology, logy

LIST 2

anthropology
mythology
pathology
technology

Ology is a Greek suffix that means "science or study of." Another way to spell this suffix is ***logy***.

- Words that end in *ology* or *logy* have something to do with the science or study of a particular subject.

When you see *ology* or *logy,* think of *meteor**ology*** (the "study of" weather).

Clues to Meaning Use *ology* and *logy* as clues to the meanings of the underlined words.

Ben Anthropology is the study of a subject, but which one?

Teacher Look at the first part of the word. *Anthropos* is a Greek root meaning "human."

Ben So anthropology is the study of humans?

Teacher It's actually the study of the history of humans.

Ben So that means mythology is the study of myths. And technology studies ways of doing things and controlling things scientifically. But what does *path* mean?

Teacher *Path* means "diseases," so what does pathology mean?

LESSON 47

LIST 3

biologist
cardiologist
geologist
psychologist

ologist, logist

Ologist is a Greek suffix that means "a person who studies or is an expert in a particular area of science." Another way to spell this suffix is ***logist***.

ANCHOR WORD
meteor**ologist**

When you see *ologist* or *logist,* think of *meteor**ologist*** (a "person who studies" weather).

Clues to Meaning Use *ologist* and *logist* as clues to the meanings of the underlined words.

Derrick When I grow up, I want to be a biologist, so I can study what living things are made of and how they grow.

Miguel I'd rather be a doctor. In fact, I think I'd make a great cardiologist. I've always been interested in how the heart works.

Sara Earth is what fascinates me—what it's made of and how it formed. A geologist would be the perfect career for me!

Mia The human mind is what I want to figure out. Why do people act, think, and feel the way they do? I can't wait to be a psychologist.

In Your Notebook Write each list word and its meaning. Add other words that describe the study of a subject and the person who studies that subject.

Mythological Allusions

Mythological allusions are references to people, places, or things mentioned in mythology. Many companies use mythological allusions in their advertising. For example, a famous florist hints at the speed of its service with a picture of Mercury, the Roman messenger god who is always pictured with wings on the heels of his sandals. And don't forget Nike, the winged goddess of victory who could run and fly at great speeds. Why do sports items refer to Nike?

Do you know these mythological allusions?

- Achilles' heel
- the Midas touch
- Pandora's box
- Cupid's arrow

Apply and Extend

List 1

Intermittent refers to breaks between actions, such as intermittent rain. Write a sentence describing another kind of intermittent action.

List 2

Write a question about one of the words in List 2, showing that you understand its meaning. An example question for the word *pathology* is: *Which word describes the study of diseases?*

List 3

Which list word interests you most as a career? Why?

Clue Review Choose a list word and give your partner a clue about it. Did your partner guess the word correctly? If not, provide another clue until your partner correctly identifies it. Then switch roles.

LESSON 48 Domain-Specific Vocabulary
Social Studies

LIST WORDS

annex
basin
colonize
coup
enclave
impact
isolationism
topography

Use Context as Clues to Meaning

Geo is a Greek prefix that means "earth." *Geology* is the study of the Earth and the processes that have formed it. A *geologist* is a person who works in that field, or profession. *Geography* is the study of the physical features of the Earth, as well as how these physical features affect and are affected by people. *Topography* is another word that describes physical features of the Earth. Topography is made up of the Greek roots *topo* and *graph.*

topo (place) + graph (to write, including drawing) = topography (written or drawn description of a place)

You may come across *geology, geologist, geography,* and *topography* as well as the other list words in your social studies class.

Read this passage from a social studies book. How does the context help you understand the meanings of the underlined words?

In addition to hills and valleys, the topography, or the features of the area, included a basin that held water year-round. When families left their countries in search of new land to settle in, plentiful water drew them to colonize an area and raise a variety of crops there. The farming families formed their own self-contained enclave because their culture differed from that of people who had been living in the surrounding hills for a long time. This isolationism gradually ended when farmers began to interact and trade with people who lived and worked outside of their farming community.

Another important impact, or effect, of trade was that people worked together to produce enough food to trade with neighboring towns. Eventually, smaller communities wanted to be annexed, or joined, to a larger town. Most of the people saw the social and economic benefits of joining, so they agreed. In fact, some of them saw it as a coup—a highly successful and clever move—on their part.

In Your Notebook Use each list word in a sentence that contains context clues to the word's meaning. If you want to check the meanings, use a dictionary.

Foreign Words in English

Several of the words on the list come from the French language. The word *coup* comes from a French word meaning "blow" or "strike." It now refers to events ranging from the overthrow of a government to a sudden, important decision or act. The word *basin* originally meant "a shallow dish or bowl." *Basin* is still used in that way, but its meaning has expanded to describe any large landscape feature that holds water. The word *annex* also comes from a French word, but originally came from a Latin word that meant "to connect with or bind."

Did you know?

The word *isolation* comes from a Latin word meaning "made into an island." *Isolationism* is the policy of keeping one's country separate from the affairs of other countries.

Apply and Extend

- The word *enclave* sometimes refers to a country or region completely surrounded by the territory of another country. For example, Vatican City, an independent city-state, lies completely within a walled enclave in Rome, Italy. *Enclave* also refers to an isolated group of people, such as Catholic cardinals who meet in secret to elect a new pope. Write one or two sentences about other groups or places that might be called an enclave.

- People from several different countries once colonized areas of the present-day United States. Name one state in the United States that was once colonized by either the English, the French, or the Spanish. Write a sentence about the founding of the colony.

Graphic Gallery Create a comic strip of the social studies passage on the previous page. Draw pictures and write dialogue in each frame. Each frame should also include one of the list words in a way that shows that you understand the meaning of the word. With your classmates, create a Graphic Gallery with your comic strips.

LIST 1

antisocial
sociable
socialist
socialized
society
sociology
sociopath
unsocial

soci

Soci is a Latin root that means "companion."

- Words containing *soci* usually have something to do with relationships.

When you see *soci,* think of ***social*** (spending time with "companions").

Clues to Meaning Use *soci* as a clue to the meanings of the underlined words.

Alex I now call to order this meeting of the Food Depot Friends, a society of volunteers who raise money for our local food bank. Welcome to Amiri, a new member of our group.

Amiri Thanks, Alex! Everyone seems to get along so well here. My last volunteer group wasn't this sociable. One member had no idea how to behave and didn't care what people thought, acting just like a sociopath!

Rosa Well, there's no one like that here, thank goodness! Some people have not been socialized very well at home. They haven't learned how to be comfortable with other people. Unsocial people aren't interested in spending time with others, and antisocial people are really against spending time in groups.

Amiri That's interesting! Where did you learn that?

Rosa I read a chapter in my sister's sociology book. It's fascinating to study how people live together in groups.

Alex Well, let's get started. Amiri, we have a kind of socialist system here. No one person tells us what to do; we all contribute to the success of the group by cooperating with one another.

Amiri Awesome! I'm so glad that I found this kind of club!

LIST 2

contract
distract
subcontract
traction

tract

Tract is a Latin root that means "pull" or "drag."

- Words containing *tract* usually have something to do with pulling or dragging.

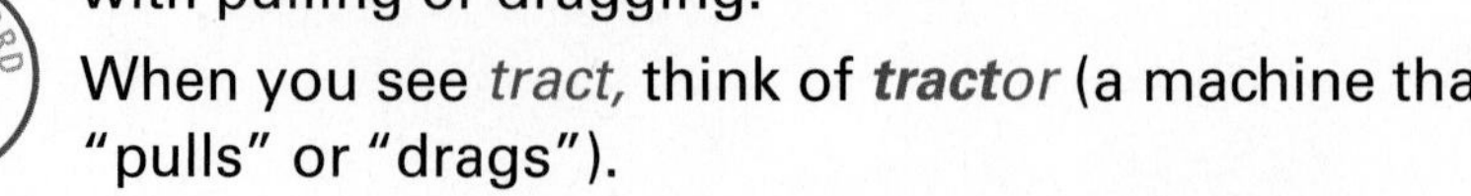

When you see *tract,* think of ***tractor*** (a machine that "pulls" or "drags").

Clues to Meaning Use *tract* as a clue to the meanings of the underlined words.

- Ray signed a contract, an agreement that he'd complete the gardening project in a month, but he didn't read the fine print. He had a lot of work to do to meet that deadline! He needed help, so he subcontracted work to another gardener, giving part of the work to her.
- The bee distracted the player. Because he couldn't pay attention to what he was doing, he lost traction in the muddy field, and his footing slipped.

In Your Notebook Write each list word and a clue to its meaning.

Prefix and Suffix Study

Word parts at the beginning of a word (prefixes) and at the end of a word (suffixes) change a root or base word to make a new word. Most of these word parts come from Greek or Latin. See how the following prefixes and suffixes, when added to the root *soci* (meaning "companion"), create new words:

Prefixes		**New Word**
un:	"not"	unsocial (not being a companion)
anti:	"against"	antisocial (against being a companion)
Suffixes		
able:	"capable of"	sociable (capable of being a companion)
al:	"of," "relating to"	social (relating to or being a companion)
ology:	"study of"	sociology (study of companionship)
ist:	"person with"	socialist (person who supports socialism, one system of political beliefs)

Knowing the meanings of prefixes and suffixes can help you figure out the meanings of the words to which they are affixed.

Apply and Extend

Have you heard these expressions?

- social butterfly
- ice cream social
- social network
- social skills

List 1

Which two words with the root *soci* are synonyms? Which two words with the root *soci* are antonyms?

List 1

People tend to be *social* in some situations and *unsocial* in other situations. Using as many list words as possible, write about a situation when you were either *social* or *unsocial*.

List 2

Choose a list word and explain how knowing the meaning of the root *tract* helps you understand the meaning of the list word. Write an explanation similar to this example:

> I understand the meaning of the word *intractable* because I know *in* means "un" or "not," *tract* means "to pull" or "to drag," and *able* means "capable of." So *intractable* means "not being capable of pulling or dragging." An intractable person is someone who has ideas that cannot be "pulled" or changed.

Act It Out Put your acting talent to work. Work with several classmates to perform a skit based on the passages in this lesson. Choose a narrator and students to play the characters in the passage. Become your character!

LIST WORDS

coefficient
cube
infinity
integer
median
meter
number line
quadrant

Use Context as Clues to Meaning

Many words used in mathematics have their beginnings in Latin and Greek. For example, the word *subtract* comes from the Latin *subtractus*, which is derived from another Latin word, *subtrahere*, which means "carry off" or "take away."

At the right are words used in mathematics. You may come across them in your math class.

Read the following sentences. How do the context and the examples help you understand the meanings of the underlined words?

- A coefficient is a number used to multiply a variable. For example, in the expression 9*a* (which means 9 times a number represented by the letter *a*), *a* is a variable, and 9 is a coefficient.
- A number's cube is that number to the third power, as in $3^3 = 3 \times 3 \times 3$; $3^3 = 27$, so the cube of 3 is 27.
- Infinity is a quantity that has no end. It is represented by the symbol ∞.
- An integer is a positive or negative whole number. Some examples of integers are 1, 2, and 3, and -1, -2, and -3.
- A median is the middle number in a series of numbers arranged from least to greatest. For example, in the series 30, 31, 33, 34, 35, 43, and 46, the middle number is 35, so the median is 35.
- A meter is the basic unit of length or distance in the metric system. One meter is equal to 39.37 inches.
- A number line is a line without ends, with numbers that are placed in correct positions in relation to zero.

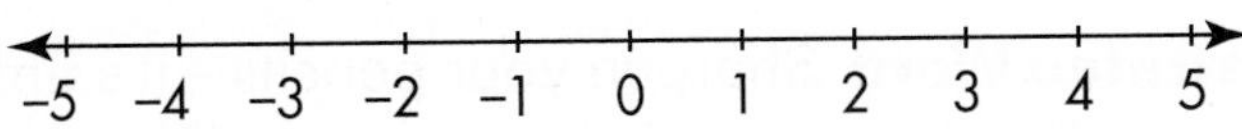

- A quadrant is one of the four parts into which a plane is divided by two perpendicular lines. The point (–2, 2) is in the second quadrant.

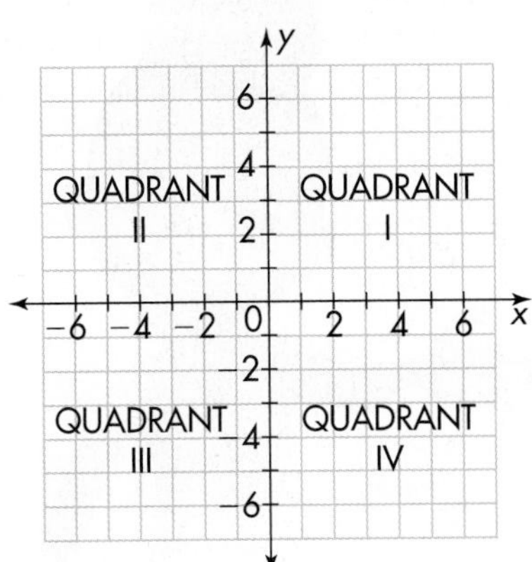

In Your Notebook Write the list words. Write or draw a clue or an example to help you remember each term.

Using a Dictionary

Keep in mind that checking a dictionary will help you find a precise meaning for words with multiple meanings.

For example, the dictionary provides several definitions for the word *infinity*. One general meaning is "an infinite distance, space, time, or quantity." (*Infinite* is defined as "greater than can be reached in counting.") This definition of *infinite* can be used to describe the universe, an idea, or a spiritual value. The dictionary also notes that the meaning of *infinity* in mathematics is "an infinite quantity," or an uncountable number.

For multiple-meaning words, check a dictionary to find the general, common meanings of the words and the different meanings they may have in a specific context, such as math.

Did you know?

The United States is the only industrialized nation that has not officially adopted the metric system. You would say, "I live a mile from school," while a student from Europe would say, "I live a kilometer from school."

Apply and Extend

- Write a riddle for one of the words. For example, *Which word can be positive or negative?* Exchange riddles with a classmate and answer each other's riddles. If there is time, continue with other list words.
- In this lesson, the word *cube* is defined as "a number to the third power." However, *cube* has other meanings. Think of another meaning for *cube* and write a sentence using this meaning. You may want to consult a dictionary.

The Illustrated Word Sharpen your pencils—it's time to play a picture game. Divide a group into two teams. Write lesson words on cards and place them in a stack upside down. The first person on Team 1 takes a card, draws a picture or writes a math example that represents the word on the card, and shows it to his or her team. If team members guess the word in 30 seconds, the team gets a point. Now it's Team 2's turn.

crit

LIST 1

criteria
critical
criticism
hypocrite

Crit is a Greek root that means "judge."

- Words containing *crit* usually have something to do with judging something.
- Use *crit* as a clue to meaning when you come across words that contain this root.

When you see *crit,* think of ***crit****ic* (a person who "judges" something, such as a book or movie).

Clues to Meaning Use *crit* as a clue to the meanings of the underlined words.

- She seems to find fault and judge me harshly whenever I try a new move in the dance. She's very critical.
- He is a hypocrite because he claims to have high principles about littering—but litters anyway! Even today he left cans on the ground.
- To qualify for the marathon, runners had to meet several criteria, or standards. The race's organizers received a lot of criticism from some runners who commented harshly, disagreeing with the marathon policies because they just wanted to run for fun.

jud

LIST 2

judgment
misjudge
prejudice

Jud is a Latin root that means "judge."

- Words containing *jud* usually have something to do with judging.

When you see *jud,* think of ***jud****ge* (a person who "judges," or makes a decision or forms an opinion).

Clues to Meaning Use *jud* as a clue to the meanings of the underlined words.

- Use your own best judgment; make good decisions when trying to decide which course of action to take.
- "I think you have misjudged me," Elena said to her friend Marco. "You're wrong to think I don't like soccer. Before I played it, I had an unfavorable opinion of it and thought it was silly. So I may have been prejudiced then. But now that I've been playing, I love it!"

LIST 3 ous

anonymous
envious
indigenous
mountainous
perilous

Ous is a Latin suffix that means "possessing" or "full of."

- To figure out the meanings of words with the suffix *ous*, identify the root or base word first and then add the meaning "possessing" or "full of."

When you see *ous,* think of *famous* ("possessing" fame).

Clues to Meaning Use *ous* as a clue to the meanings of the underlined words.

- George was envious of the anonymous writer who had left the unsigned note in his backpack. He was jealous because he wishes he could use language as creatively as that person; but with no name on the note, he didn't know who wrote it.
- Although some explorers had attempted to climb the cliffs, the journey was very perilous, and most of them turned back because of the danger.
- A region cannot be called "mountainous" if there are no mountains.
- The indigenous people were the original inhabitants of the land.

In Your Notebook Write each list word and its meaning. What context clues helped you figure out word meanings?

Etymology Study

Sometimes you can figure out a word's meaning if you look at its history, or etymology. The word *hypocrite* has two Greek roots, *hypo*, which means "under," and *crit*, which means "judge." The Greek word *hupokritēs* meant literally "under a judge," or under assessment, probably because an actor had to decide how to act out a role in a play. The Greek word came to mean a "stage actor" or "one who plays a part." Because of that, *hupokritēs* came to mean "pretender." A hypocrite, then, is a person who pretends to be something he or she is not.

Apply and Extend

■ List 1

The words *critic, critical*, and *criticism* are closely related. Use the three words in one sentence.

■ List 2

Explain how the meanings of the words *judgment, misjudge*, and *prejudice* differ.

■ List 3

Envious is a feeling meaning "full of envy." Choose three other list words and tell how each has to do with being "full."

Clue Review Choose a list word and give your partner a clue about it. Draw a sketch, if appropriate, and offer that as a clue. Did your partner guess the word correctly? If not, provide another clue until your partner correctly identifies the word. Then switch roles.

Did you know?

The list word *indigenous* comes from Latin words meaning "in" and "to give birth." Being indigenous to a place means having been born there.

LESSON 52 General Academic Vocabulary

The Right Word for the Right Context

LIST WORDS

analyze
cogitate
contemplate
elaboration
hypothesis
mull
ponder
theorize

Use Context as Clues to Meaning

Someone who expresses his or her thoughts about, or judges the merits or faults of, books, music, pictures, plays, acting, and so on, is a *critic*. He or she might write a *critique* (from the Greek root *crit*, which means "judge"), or review, of a book, movie, or video game—or even a political speech. Would a critic be more likely to *analyze* or *theorize?* To *contemplate* or *cogitate?* All of these words deal with *thinking*. You will learn their meanings in this lesson.

Read the following paragraphs. How does the context help you understand the meanings of the underlined words?

In 1961, President John F. Kennedy theorized that the United States could land a person on the moon within a decade. Kennedy formed this idea on the fact that Americans had the know-how to reach this amazing goal. His hypothesis, or educated guess, was that the only thing that stood between imagination and success was a lack of commitment.

Kennedy was very persuasive, and Americans began to contemplate, or carefully consider, the possibility of traveling in space. Kennedy spoke in great detail about his vision, and his elaboration of his ideas helped Congress understand them. Members of Congress began to ponder a budget for such an extraordinarily difficult and complex program, thinking about what funds might be available. Scientists cogitated, or thought deeply, about the technical aspects of the project and the safest and most efficient way to proceed. They also had to consider and mull over various ways to accomplish their task. NASA, the National Aeronautics and Space Administration, began to analyze, or carefully examine, the steps necessary to make the dream of people traveling to the moon and back a reality.

In Your Notebook Write each list word. Then write about a time when you thought deeply about something. Use two or three of the list words to describe your thought process.

Using an Online Dictionary

Some of the words in this lesson are synonyms—words with the same or similar meanings. How can you determine or clarify the precise meaning of a word? Use an online dictionary.

- Enter a vocabulary word and the word *definition* in a search engine.
- Read through each definition.
- Try each meaning in the sentence you are reading.
- Choose the definition that makes the most sense in that sentence.

For example, the list words *mull* and *ponder* are synonyms. Both mean "to consider." However, the precise meaning of *mull* is "to think about without making much progress." The phrase "without making much progress" distinguishes *mull* from *ponder*.

Did you know?

The words *cogitate* and *cognition* are both about thinking but have different roots. *Cogitate* means "think over." It has the Latin root *co*, which means "intensive." *Cognition* means "awareness." It has the Latin root *cogn*, which means "to know" or "to learn."

Apply and Extend

- Think about a decision you made recently. How did you make the decision? Write a few sentences using list words to explain your thought process.
- The word *contemplate* has multiple meanings. In this lesson, *contemplate* means "to carefully consider." Look up a second meaning of the word in an online dictionary. Then use *contemplate* in a sentence, demonstrating a different meaning for the word.

Skit What is one invention or solution that helped change the world? Think about the words in this lesson. Work with a partner or small group to perform a skit that uses or is based on some of these words.

LESSON 53 Word Parts and Meanings

spec, spic, carn

LIST 1

conspicuous
inspector
prospect
specimen
spectacular
speculate
suspicion
suspicious

spec, spic

Spec is a Latin root that means "look." Another way to spell this root is *spic.*

- Words containing *spec* or *spic* usually have something to do with looking.
- Use *spec* or *spic* as a clue to meaning when you come across words that contain this root.

When you see *spec* or *spic,* think of ***spec****tacle* (something impressive that people "look" at).

Clues to Meaning Use *spec* and *spic* as clues to the meanings of the underlined words.

Have you ever read Sir Arthur Conan Doyle's stories about the famous detective Sherlock Holmes and his sidekick, Dr. Watson? Holmes is often brought in on a case that baffles local inspectors, police officers who have looked at the evidence but are unable to solve the mystery. Fans of Sherlock Holmes enjoy looking ahead and thinking about the prospect of a spectacular, or stunning, end to the case, when people can see, understand, and admire his exciting discovery.

When he is called in on a case, Holmes first looks for clues, including specimens of physical evidence, at the crime scene. These samples are sometimes conspicuous, but Holmes also finds evidence that is not so easy to see. Once he has found the clues, he speculates, carefully considering what each one means. He is suspicious of everyone, thinking that even those who appear to be innocent might be guilty. Other characters in the stories are often shocked by his suspicions, especially when his beliefs turn out to be correct.

LIST 2

carnage
carnival
carnivorous
incarnation

carn

Carn is a Latin root that means "flesh."

- Words containing *carn* usually have something to do with flesh or eating meat.

When you see *carn,* think of ***carn****ivore* (a person or animal who eats "flesh," or meat).

Clues to Meaning Use *carn* as a clue to the meanings of the underlined words.

- The carnival won't be here all year. At the end of the summer, they pack up the different rides and shows and travel to a different state.
- I don't think I could be a vegetarian. I'm carnivorous—I like to eat meat.
- After reading about the killing of the vast numbers of animals, I was astounded by the carnage.
- When she dances, she embodies and exhibits elegance and beauty. She is the incarnation of grace.

In Your Notebook Write a definition for each list word in your own words. Then check your definitions in a dictionary.

Antonym Study

An antonym is a word that means the opposite of another word. For example, take the list word *conspicuous*. It has the Latin root *con,* which means "with" or "together," and *spic,* which means "look." Something that is conspicuous is seen easily "with looking." Some antonyms for *conspicuous* are *inconspicuous, invisible, unclear,* and *obscure*.

What antonyms can you think of for other words in this lesson?

Apply and Extend

List 1

Using the word *speculate* or any form of the word, write a sentence about one of your theories or opinions.

List 1

The word *inspector* has more than one meaning. Write two sentences, each using a different meaning of *inspector*.

List 2

With a partner, take turns asking and answering three questions each with words that have the Latin root *carn*. An example is: *What is one kind of animal that is carnivorous?*

Did you know?

In Spanish and Portuguese, the word *carne* means "meat." *Chile con carne* (literally, "chile with meat" —a stew of beans, meat, chili peppers, and other ingredients) is a Mexican dish that is popular in the United States.

Rap It Up With a classmate, choose one or more list words. Use each word and its definition to create a short poem or rap, such as the one below. Compile it with other students' raps in a Rap It Up notebook.

Carnivals and Carnivores

Hey, ho, the carnival is here this year.
Rides, games, bright lights, and Big Top—Stop!
Got a craving for some *Carne-on-a-Stick*—
That's Spanish, y'all, for meat!
Yes, no mistaking, I'm carnivorous—
Don't dig vegetables, they make me shiver—Shush!
'Specially broccoli, tastes like—Mush!
Just serve up the meat!—and Hush!

LIST WORDS

antagonist
denouement
diction
multimedia
protagonist
resolution
rubric
stanza

Use Context as Clues to Meaning

Theater, one of the oldest art forms, was an important part of ancient Greek culture. Many words about theater have Greek roots. At the right are words related to the theater. You may come across these words in your language arts class.

A protagonist is the main character in a story. The word *protagonist* has two Greek roots (*proto* and *agon*) and the Greek suffix *ist*.

proto (first) + agon (struggle) + ist (one who does) = protagonist (someone who takes the first or leading part in a struggle)

Antagonists are characters who oppose the protagonist. The word *antagonist* has two Greek roots (*anti* and *agon*) and the Greek suffix *ist*.

anti (against) + agon (struggle) + ist (one who does) = antagonist (someone who fights or struggles against another)

Read the passage below. How does the context help you understand the meanings of the underlined words?

Mr. Lee Let's plan our class show, "The Great Greeks."

Raul Pedro and I are performing a scene from a Greek play. I'm the protagonist, the leading character—the hero.

Pedro And I'm the antagonist—the foe, or antihero. I'll do everything I can to prevent Raul's character from achieving his goals.

Michelle I'm going to read a couple of stanzas from a poem. Each one has four lines with a repeated rhyme scheme. I have practiced my diction and can pronounce all the words very clearly.

Leo Judy and I have been practicing the final scene from another play. In its denouement, or ending, there is a resolution in which all of the play's conflicts are untangled and worked out.

Rosario A few of us are working on a multimedia presentation about Greek theater, with music, computer graphics, and Greek art.

Mr. Lee Spectacular! I'm impressed! Now, let's talk about the rubric for the project. We need to create a list of procedures and protocols so everyone will be clear about the expectations for the project.

In Your Notebook Write each list word and a brief clue that will help you remember the word.

Literary Allusions

The words in this lesson relate to the theater, a place where you might encounter literary allusions. A literary allusion is a direct or indirect reference to a well-known character, place, or event in literature. For example, when someone says that he or she downloaded a "Trojan horse," that person is alluding to the Trojan horse in the *Iliad*. The Greeks were able to trick the Trojans by entering the city of Troy hidden in a large wooden horse. On a computer, a Trojan horse is software that a user is tricked into downloading. It usually runs a program that will harm the computer.

Look for literary allusions in what you see, hear, and read. They can help you see connections between ideas or help you better understand the subject.

Did you know?

The origin of the word *denouement* is *denouer*, which means "untie." The *denouement* in a play is when the conflicts are resolved, or "untied."

Apply and Extend

- Find a poem in a book or online. How many stanzas does it have? What rhyme pattern do the stanzas have? Try writing a stanza with a similar pattern.
- Write the names of a protagonist and an antagonist in a play, novel, or movie, and tell what makes each character a protagonist or an antagonist.

Skit Would you like to plan a performance like "The Great Greeks" show? Think about the words in this lesson. Work with a partner or small group to write and perform a skit that uses or is based on some of these words. The show can be about music, movies, or theater, or about a historical or cultural subject. The sky's the limit!

aud

LIST 1

audible
audiovisual
audition
auditorium

Aud is a Latin root that means "hear."

- Words containing *aud* usually have something to do with hearing.

When you see *aud,* think of ***aud**ience* (a group of people who "hear" a performance).

Clues to Meaning Use *aud* as a clue to the meanings of the underlined words.

Bo entered the <u>auditorium</u>, ready to perform her song for the <u>audition</u>. She looked around the large room and saw many people waiting to try out for the play. Mrs. Ray had reminded us to sing loudly so that we would be <u>audible</u>. And she had announced that <u>auditions</u> would be taped so that she could review the <u>audiovisual</u> record. Seeing and hearing the singers on tape would help her choose the cast.

phon

LIST 2

homophone
microphone
phonics

Phon is a Greek root that means "sound."

- Use *phon* as a clue to meaning when you come across words that contain this root.

When you see *phon,* think of *sym**phon**y* (many instruments playing together to make a unique "sound").

Clues to Meaning Use *phon* as a clue to the meanings of the underlined words.

Ms. Marlin passed out these instructions at the regional spelling bee.

1. Adjust the <u>microphone</u> to your height, so you can speak into it. This will help the people in the back of the room hear you.
2. Remember to focus on the sounds of the individual letters, syllables, and words, as you learned to do when you studied <u>phonics</u>.
3. Ask for context for <u>homophones</u>, words that sound the same but have different spellings, such as *ate* and *eight*.
4. Don't rush. Take your time. And have fun!

LESSON 55

LIST 3

clearance
coincidence
disturbance
persistence
substance

ance, ence

Ance is a Latin suffix that means "action," "process," or "state." Another way to spell this suffix is ***ence***.

- Words containing *ance* or *ence* usually have something to do with an action, process, or state. When you see *ance* or *ence,* think of *annoy****ance*** (the "state" of being annoyed).

Clues to Meaning Use *ance* and *ence* as clues to the meanings of the underlined words.

Jill I'm going to help my uncle with the <u>clearance</u> sale at his store. He's selling everything at half price to make room for new items.

Scott I was thinking of going too! What a <u>coincidence</u> that we're going to be at the same place without having planned it that way!

Scully Be careful in that shopping center. A robbery caused quite a <u>disturbance</u> last week, with alarms and sirens blaring and streets being closed. What a commotion! I wonder if they caught the thieves.

Jill Well, police found a strange, chalky <u>substance</u> near a broken window. They're checking that stuff for the robbers' fingerprints.

Scott Investigations take a lot of <u>persistence</u>. Despite any challenges, the detectives keep trying until they solve the crime.

In Your Notebook Write each list word and its meaning. What context clues helped you figure out those word meanings?

Synonym Study

A synonym is a word with the same or nearly the same meaning as another word. Some words have many synonyms, and some of those words have slightly different shades of meaning.

The list word *disturbance* means a "state" of being disturbed. When a disturbance is defined as an event, synonyms include *disorder* and *commotion*. For emotional disturbances, synonyms include *confusion, uneasiness,* and *worry*. Remember to choose and use the precise word in your writing in order to convey the exact meaning you wish to communicate.

Did you know?

People sometimes mix up the homophones *they're* (the contraction for *they are*), *their* (a possessive pronoun), and *there*. Try this sentence to help you remember the differences: *They're looking for their coats over there!*

Apply and Extend

List 1

Write an announcement for an audition. Use other words on this list.

List 2

Think of more examples of homophones. Then write sentences using both (or more) meanings in the same sentence.

List 3

Identify the three list words with base words that can stand on their own. Then find the meanings of the roots for the other two words.

Act It Out Work with several classmates to perform a skit based on the story of Bo's audition. Choose a narrator and students to play the characters in the passage. Use as many of the list words in your skit as you can.

LESSON 56 Domain-Specific Vocabulary

Science

LIST WORDS

absorption
evaporation
moisture
ozone
pollution
precipitation
stratosphere
ultraviolet

Use Context as Clues to Meaning

Many scientists have warned us that humans are having a negative effect on Earth's environment. Some people believe that recent large-scale weather events and Earth's rising temperatures are simply coincidences. At the left are words used to describe weather and the environment. You may come across these words in your science class.

Read the following passage. How does the context help you understand the underlined words and what is happening to the environment?

Scientists are concerned about climate change and the impact of human actions on the Earth. One problem concerns water. In the water cycle, precipitation, in the form of rain or snow, falls to the Earth. With evaporation, some of that water is changed into small particles of water, or moisture, which rise into the air. Unfortunately, the water cycle around the world has become unstable, making weather unpredictable—and sometimes destructive. Some consequences of large-scale changes in the weather are more widespread drought, flooding, and extreme storms.

Another environmental problem concerns the layer of ozone gas around the Earth. Most ozone is found in the stratosphere, the level of the atmosphere extending from about 10 to 35 miles above the Earth's surface. Like a sponge, ozone absorbs dangerous ultraviolet rays from the Sun. (Ultraviolet rays are invisible rays with wavelengths shorter than those of violet light. In sunlight, they are important for forming vitamin D, but can cause sunburn.) There is an expanding hole in the layer of ozone around the Earth, so the absorption of ultraviolet rays is being reduced, and more of those rays are reaching the Earth.

A major reason the ozone layer is breaking down is pollution, especially dirty air that is caused when people burn fossil fuels, such as gasoline. Humans have contributed to infecting and contaminating many parts of the environment. Fortunately, pollution of our planet is something we can all do something about.

In Your Notebook Write each list word and its meaning. If possible, use illustrations to further define some of the words.

Etymology Study

One of the things that makes language interesting is learning where words come from—their etymology. Even more interesting is learning how word meaning and usage change over time. For example, take *evaporation*. The Latin root of *evaporation* is *vapor,* which means "steam." *Evaporation* has a fairly straightforward definition: turning water from liquid into gas. During the Victorian era, some doctors believed that melancholy feelings were "vapors" that rose up through the body and affected the mind. This condition was supposedly experienced only by women. Today the word is used primarily in its literal sense—changing liquid into gas. However, the idea of evaporation is occasionally used in fictional space adventures, in which enemies can "vaporize," or destroy each other, with special weapons!

Did you know?

There's nothing like the sweet smell in the air after it rains. But sometimes the smell isn't very sweet at all! What you are smelling then is ozone. *Ozone* comes from *ozein,* a Greek root meaning "to smell."

Apply and Extend

- Using the words *absorption, evaporation, moisture,* and *precipitation,* write two or three sentences that explain how water can move or change.
- Create an anti-pollution flyer warning others of the dangers of pollution. Use as many words as possible from the word list.

Clue Review Play a word game with one of your classmates. Choose one of the list words. Give your partner a clue about the word. Did your partner guess the word correctly? If not, provide another clue until your partner correctly identifies the word. Then switch roles.

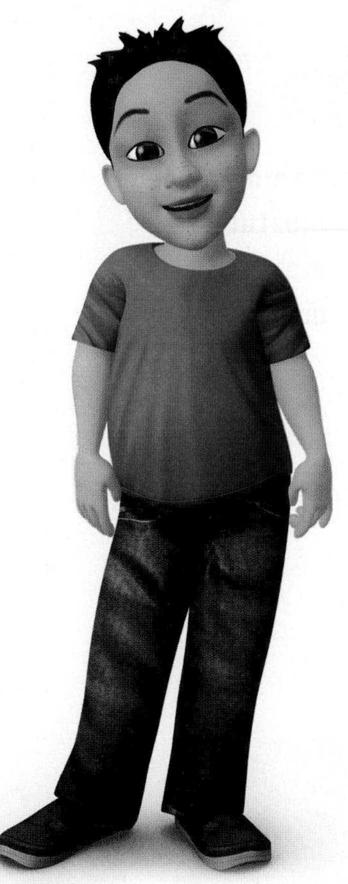

LESSON 57 Word Parts and Meanings

bio, mort, anti

LIST 1 bio

biodiversity
bionic
biopsy
biotechnology

Bio is a Greek root that means "life."

- Words containing *bio* usually have something to do with life.

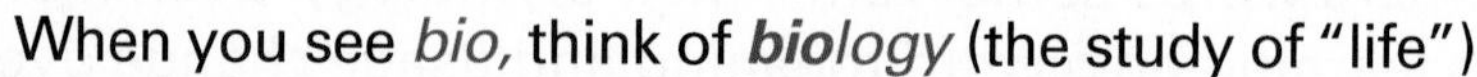

When you see *bio,* think of ***bio**logy* (the study of "life").

Clues to Meaning Use *bio* as a clue to the meanings of the underlined words.

Inara The exhibit on <u>biodiversity</u> was informative. I never knew there was such a variety of plant and animal life in the world.

Joss And what about that special exhibit on <u>biotechnology</u>?

Inara I had no idea that scientists could apply technology to biology in such creative ways—like creating <u>bionic</u> limbs for humans. They showed an arm that had both biological and electronic parts.

Joss Did it show how <u>biotechnology</u> can be used in a <u>biopsy</u>? That's a laboratory test in which a patient's tissue is examined so that a doctor can make a diagnosis.

LIST 2 mort

immortalize
mortal
mortality
mortician

Mort is a Latin root that means "death."

- Words containing *mort* usually have something to do with death.

When you see *mort,* think of *im**mort**al* (living forever without "death").

Clues to Meaning Use *mort* as a clue to the meanings of the underlined words.

- Many young people do not think that they are <u>mortal</u> and will someday die.
- As people grow older, they become more aware of their <u>mortality</u>—the knowledge that they will die—and that life is short.
- The <u>mortician</u> in a funeral home takes care of people's bodies after they die and comforts their families.
- Some people try to <u>immortalize</u> themselves through art. They know their art will be a reminder of them for a long time after their death.

anti

LIST 3

antibiotic
antiestablishment
antiperspirant
antiwar

Anti is a Greek prefix that means "against."

- To figure out words with the prefix *anti,* identify the root or base word first and then add the meaning "against."

When you see *anti,* think of ***anti****smoking* ("against" smoking).

Clues to Meaning Use *anti* as a clue to the meanings of the underlined words.

- Margo wished she had remembered to wear antiperspirant on her underarms. It was a hot day, and she was sweating more than usual.
- Put antibiotic ointment on cuts to prevent an infection by bacteria.
- Protesters in the U.S. antiwar movement used public gatherings to pressure the government to end the Vietnam War. Many protestors made antiestablishment speeches, speaking against the government.

In Your Notebook Use each list word in a sentence that contains at least one context clue to the word's meaning. To check a meaning, use a dictionary.

Analogy Study

Forming an analogy is one way of comparing or contrasting words or ideas. An analogy is a sentence that has two word pairs, with the same relationship between the items in each pair. Identify the relationship between the first pair of words in order to see a relationship between the second pair. The two words in a pair might be synonyms, antonyms, or parts of a whole. Here's an example of an analogy:

Antibiotic is to disease as antiperspirant is to ______.

An antibiotic fights and eliminates disease. What does an antiperspirant eliminate? Sweat! So "sweat" goes in the blank. Creating analogies is an interesting way to think about words!

Have you heard these expressions?

- shuffle off this mortal coil
- mortal combat

Apply and Extend

List 1

Which list word is the most interesting to you? Why?

List 2

The words *mortal, mortality,* and *immortalize* are closely related. Use the three words in one sentence, and include context for each word.

List 3

What are people "against" in each list word? Explain.

Act It Out Work with several classmates to perform a skit based on the passages in this lesson. Choose a narrator and students to play the characters in the passage.

LIST WORDS

amendment
bylaw
census
deficit
innovation
interest
investment
merchant

Use Context as Clues to Meaning

The word *antismoking* includes the prefix *anti,* meaning "against." Someone who is *antismoking* believes that people should not smoke. Around the United States, state and federal antismoking laws keep Americans from smoking in public places. At the right are words related to the ways in which laws are made in the United States.

Read about some of the ways the U.S. government gathers information and considers creating new laws or revising existing laws. How does the context help you understand the meanings of the underlined words?

- A census is an official count of the people in a country. The 2010 U.S. census showed that the country's population is growing very rapidly. This survey also provides information about the U.S. economy.
- Merchants buy goods at one price and make money by selling the products to customers at a higher price. To be successful, merchants have to sell products that people want and sell them at reasonable, but competitive, prices.
- Everyone seems to agree that we need to reduce the nation's budget deficit. But how can the government fix the problem of spending more money than it takes in? Some people think that the United States should spend money on innovations. Developing something new and different, such as advanced technology, will be an investment that we're sure to profit from in the future, they say. However, many legislators are concerned about the interest on our national debt. This fee for borrowing money that we owe to lenders is growing very quickly.
- Even when people agree on basic ideas, they often disagree about the details. Lawmakers often attach amendments to proposed laws, hoping that these additions will improve those laws.
- Corporations and local organizations can adopt bylaws, or rules, to regulate the affairs or actions of its members.

In Your Notebook Write each list word and its meaning. Note what context clues helped you figure out each definition. To check a meaning, use a dictionary.

LESSON 58

Multiple Meanings

English contains many words that have more than one meaning. Often, you can figure out a specific meaning of a word by studying the context, or how the word is used, in a sentence or paragraph.

An example of a word with multiple meanings is *interest*. You might first think that it means "curiosity" as in the sentence "The new teacher was of *interest* to the students." But in the passage on the previous page (in the third bulleted paragraph), *interest* means the fee that a borrower has to pay a lender. The context clues "*interest* on our national debt" and "This fee for borrowing money that we owe" give you clues as to which meaning of *interest* is being used.

Did you know?

The words *amendment, amend,* and *mend* are related. They all have to do with "changing" or "fixing" something and have their origins in the Latin word *emendare,* which means "to fix a fault."

Apply and Extend

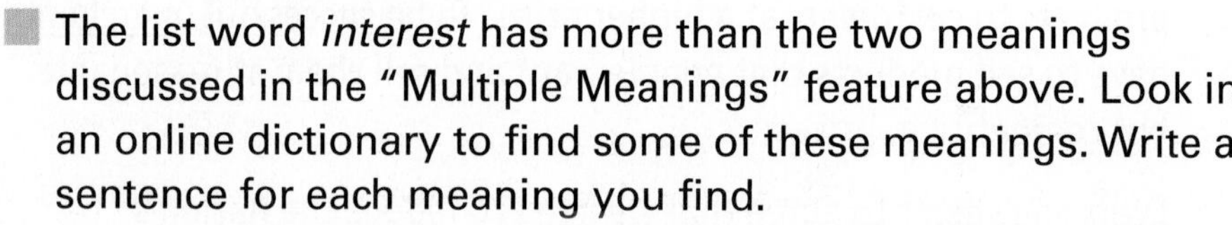

- The list word *interest* has more than the two meanings discussed in the "Multiple Meanings" feature above. Look in an online dictionary to find some of these meanings. Write a sentence for each meaning you find.
- Write a riddle about a list word. Here's an example: *Which list word would want to sell you something?* Exchange riddles with a partner and answer each other's riddles.

Graphic Gallery Use your skills as a cartoonist to create a comic strip using words from this week's lesson. Draw pictures and write dialogue or use an online program to create the graphic text. How many of the words can you use? Work together with classmates to compile the class's comic strips into a Graphic Gallery.

nomin, nomen — LIST 1

denomination
nomenclature
nominal
nominative

Nomin is a Latin root that means "name." Another spelling for this root is ***nomen***.

- Words containing *nomin* or *nomen* usually have to do with names or naming something.

When you see *nomin* or *nomen,* think of ***nomin**ate* (to "name" a candidate for a position).

Clues to Meaning Use *nomin* and *nomen* as clues to the meanings of the underlined words.

- We learned about nominatives in class. These are words, such as *who* or *I,* that act as the subject of the verb in a sentence.
- What is the denomination, or religious group, that attends the church near your house?
- Often the person who discovers a new genus of dinosaur names it. However, the International Commission on Zoological Nomenclature must first approve the name.
- Morris is the president of the Puzzle Club in name only. He is the nominal president while others do the real work.

inter — LIST 2

intercept
interjection
intermission
intertwine

Inter is a Latin prefix that means "between."

When you see *inter,* think of ***inter**viewer* (person "between" a person being asked questions and an audience).

Clues to Meaning Use *inter* as a clue to the meanings of the underlined words.

Tragic plays like *Romeo* and *Juliet* have several things in common. For instance, a character often intercepts a letter, coming between the sender and the recipient. When the message does not get through, the intended recipient often makes a fatal mistake. The characters' lives are intertwined, a twisted and tangled relationship full of misunderstandings. There is an interjection of humor thrown in from time to time to break the serious mood. During the intermission, the audience may use the break to predict how the play will end.

LIST 3

intramural
intranet
intrapersonal
intravenous

intra

Intra is a Latin prefix that means "within."

- To figure out words with the prefix *intra,* identify the root or base word first and then add the meaning "within."

When you see *intra,* think of ***intra**state* ("within" a state).

Clues to Meaning Use *intra* as a clue to the meanings of the underlined words.

- Sometimes people in the hospital need to be fed medicine intravenously, or through their veins.
- When Hector is stressed, he practices intrapersonal communication. Talking to himself has always calmed him down.
- Our school has an intranet, a computer network made specifically for members within the school to communicate with one another.
- Many students participate in the school's intramural sports programs. No one outside of the school is allowed to participate.

In Your Notebook Write each list word and its meaning. What context clues helped you figure out the words' meanings? To check a meaning, use a dictionary.

Word Roots

The word *interject* refers to introducing something suddenly into a conversation. The first part of the word *interject* comes from the Latin prefix *inter* that means "between." The second part of the word, *ject,* derives from the Latin word *jacere,* meaning "to throw."

Apply and Extend

List 1

Choose two words. For each one, write a sentence to show you understand the meaning of the word.

List 2

The word *intercept* can be used in a variety of scenarios, such as sports, math, and communications. Find out its different meanings. Then write two sentences using the word in different situations.

List 3

Explain the meanings of the list words by saying something that they don't include in their definitions. For example, an *intranet* is not for the public to use to communicate.

Clue Review Play a word game with one of your classmates. Choose one of the list words. Give your partner a clue about the word. Did your partner guess the word correctly? If not, provide another clue until your partner correctly identifies the word. Then switch roles.

LESSON 60 Domain-Specific Vocabulary

Mathematics

LIST WORDS

cylinder
hexagon
polygon
polyhedron
pyramid
ray
rhombus
scale drawing

Use Context as Clues to Meaning

The word *intercept* includes the Latin prefix *inter,* meaning "between." In math, to intercept is to mark or cut off part of a line, space, surface, or solid. At the left are more words related to geometry, a branch of mathematics. You may come across these words in your math class.

Read the descriptions and study the figures. How does the context help you understand the meanings of the underlined terms?

A hexagon is a shape with six straight sides.

A rhombus is a figure with four sides. The opposite sides and opposite angles are equal.

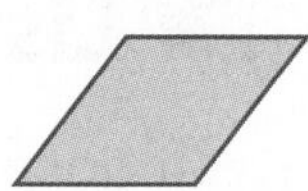

A polygon, such as a hexagon or rhombus, is a plane shape with straight sides.

A cylinder is a solid with two equal, parallel circles and a curved surface.

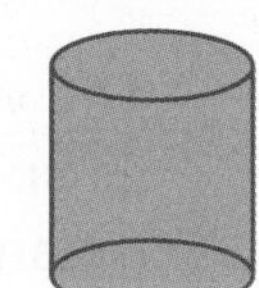

A polyhedron, such as a pyramid, is a figure with four or more faces. A pyramid has a base and triangular sides that meet at the top.

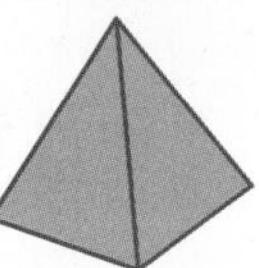

A ray is a line with a start point but no end point.

A scale drawing shows a reduced or enlarged copy of an object. The shape is the same, but the size is not.

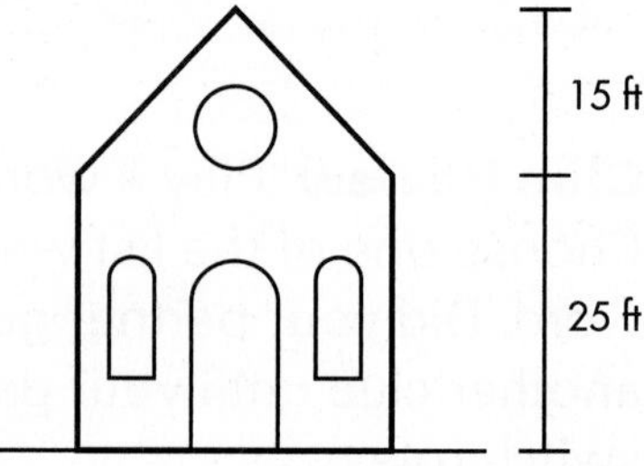

In Your Notebook Write each list word. Cover the illustration for each word and then draw your own figure, based on the description.

Context Clues

To figure out or verify the meaning of an unfamiliar word, use context clues, or text near the word that hints at the word's meaning.

In math, context clues often include definitions that give the meaning of a word and start with *is* or *or*. Example clues are equations, expressions, or illustrations that depict a word. An example is:

A hexagon is one type of polygon, or plane shape with straight sides. A hexagon has six straight sides.

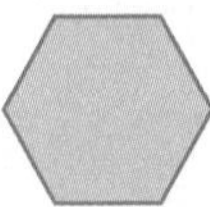

The word *or* introduces the definition clue for polygon. The figure is an example clue for hexagon.

Did you know?

The word *cylinder* comes from the Greek word *kylindein,* which means "to roll." Ancient Greeks would move heavy objects on wooden rollers. Anything shaped like a round log was also called a roller.

Apply and Extend

- The word *ray* has other meanings in addition to its meaning in math. Write two sentences with *ray,* using different meanings for the word. Use a dictionary to check the meanings.

- Review the list words and figures. How many of the figures have the same shapes as things we see or use on a regular basis, such as a can of soup (cylinder)? Write two sentences using the list words, describing the figures to someone who has never seen them.

The Illustrated Word Sharpen your pencils—it's time to play a picture game. Divide a group into two teams. Write lesson words on cards and place them in a stack upside down. The first person on Team 1 takes a card, draws a picture that represents the word on the card, and shows the picture to his or her team. If team members guess the word in 30 seconds, the team gets a point. Now it's Team 2's turn.

How to Use This Glossary

This glossary can help you understand and pronounce the words in this book. The entries in this glossary are in alphabetical order. There are guide words at the top of each page to show you the first and last words on the page. A pronunciation key is at the bottom of the following page.

1 2 3

glos·sar·y (glos′ ər ē), *n.* list of special, technical, or hard words, usually in alphabetical order, with explanations or comments: *a glossary of terms used in chemistry. Textbooks sometimes have glossaries at the end. n., pl.* **glos·sar·ies.** — 5

4

6

[**Glossary** comes from a Greek word meaning "tongue." The Greeks used *tongue* to mean "a language." Eventually this Greek word came to mean "an explanation" of hard words.]

1 *The entry word is in dark type. It shows how the word is spelled and how the word is divided into syllables.*

2 *The pronunciation is in parentheses. It also shows which syllables are stressed.*

3 *The part-of-speech label shows the function of an entry word and any listed form of that word.*

4 *The definition and examples show you what the word means and how it is used.*

5 *Inflected, irregular, and other special forms are shown to help you use the word correctly.*

6 *The etymology is in brackets and gives the origin of the entry word.*

Aa

ab·duct (ab dukt′), *v.* to carry off a person by force or by trickery; kidnap. **–ab·duc′tion,** *n.* **–ab·duc′tor,** *n.*

absolute value, *n.* the value of a real number, disregarding any arithmetical sign. The absolute value of +5, or of –5, is 5.

ab·sorp·tion (ab sôrp′shən), *n.* **1.** act or process of taking in or sucking up liquids: *A sponge picks up spilled water by absorption.* **2.** great interest: *The children's absorption in their game was so complete that they did not hear the doorbell.*

ac·cess (ak′ses), *n.* **1.** right to approach, enter, or use; admittance: *All students have access to the library during the afternoon.* **2.** approach to places, persons, or things; accessibility: *Access to mountain towns is often difficult because of poor roads.*

ac·claim (ə klām′), **1.** *v.* to welcome with loud approval; praise highly; applaud: *The crowd acclaimed the winning team.* **2.** *n.* a shout or show of approval by a crowd; applause: *His new symphony was received with great acclaim.*

ac·knowl·edge·ment (ak nol′ij mənt), *n.* **1.** something given or done to show that you have received a service, favor, gift, message, etc.: *The winner waved in acknowledgement of the cheers.* **2.** act of admitting that something is true: *acknowledgement of a mistake.*

ac·ro·pho·bi·a (ak′rə fō′bē ə), *n.* an abnormal fear of being in high places.

ad·di·tive (ad′ə tiv), **1.** *n.* substance added to another substance to preserve it, increase its effectiveness, etc. **2.** *adj.* involving addition. **–ad′di·tive·ly,** *adv.*

ad·ver·sar·y (ad′vər ser′ē), *n.* **1.** person or group opposing or hostile to another person or group; enemy: *The two countries were adversaries in World War II.* **2.** person or group on the other side in a game or contest; opponent. *n., pl.* **ad·ver·sar·ies.**

ad·vo·cate (ad′və kāt *for verb;* ad′və kit *or* ad′və kāt *for noun*), **1.** *v.* to speak or write in favor of; recommend publicly; support: *He advocates building more public housing.* **2.** *n.* person who pleads or argues for; supporter. *She is an advocate of lower property taxes. v.* **ad·vo·cat·ed, ad·vo·cat·ing. ad′vo·ca′tion,** *n.* **–ad′vo·ca′tor,** *n.*

aer·o·pho·bi·a (er′ô fō′bē ə), *n.* an abnormal fear of flying.

af·fil·i·ation (ə fil′ē ā′shən), *n.* the state or process of being joined or connected in close association.

ag·gres·sion (ə gresh′ən), *n.* **1.** the first step in an attack or a quarrel; unprovoked attack: *A country that sends its army to occupy another country is guilty of aggression.* **2.** practice of making assaults or attacks on the rights or territory of others as a method or policy.

ag·or·a·pho·bi·a (ag′ər ə fō′bē ə), *n.* an abnormal fear of open spaces.

al·ly (al′ī *or* ə lī′ *for noun;* ə lī′ *for verb*), **1.** *n.* person, group, or nation united with another for some special purpose: *England and France were allies in some wars and enemies in others.* **2.** *n.* helper; supporter. **3.** *v.* to combine for some special purpose; unite by agreement. Small nations sometimes ally themselves with larger ones for protection. *n., pl.* **al·lies;** *v.* **al·lied, al·ly·ing.**

am·ble (am′bəl), **1.** *n.* an easy, slow pace in walking. **2.** *v.* to walk at an easy, slow pace. *v.* **am·bled, am·bling. –am′bler,** *n.*

a·mend·ment (ə mend′mənt), *n.* **1.** change made in a law, bill, or motion by addition, omission, or alteration of language: *The Constitution of the United States has over twenty amendments.* **2.** a change for the better; improvement.

an·a·gram (an′ə gram), *n.* **1.** word or phrase formed from another by rearranging the letters. EXAMPLE: roved—drove. **2. anagrams,** *sing.* game in which the players make words by changing and adding letters: *Anagrams is an interesting game.*

an·a·lyze (an′l īz), *v.* **1.** to separate anything into its parts or elements to find out what it is made of: *The chemistry teacher analyzed water into two colorless gases, oxygen and hydrogen.* **2.** to examine carefully and in detail: *analyze a situation. The newspaper analyzed the results of the election. v.* **an·a·lyzed, an·a·lyz·ing. –an′a·lyz′a·ble,** *adj.* **–an′a·lyz′er,** *n.*

an·ar·chist (an′ər kist), *n.* **1.** person who wants to destroy government and laws. **2.** person who promotes disorder and stirs up revolt.

an·ar·chy (an′ər kē), *n.* **1.** absence of a system of government and law. **2.** disorder and confusion; lawlessness. [**Anarchy** comes from Greek words meaning "without" and "ruler."]

an·ces·tor (an′ses′tər), *n.* **1.** person from whom you are descended, such as your great-grandparents: *Their ancestors came to the United States in 1812.* **2.** the early form from which a species or group is descended: *Dinosaurs and snakes have the same ancestor.* [**Ancestor** comes from a Latin word meaning "to go before." Our ancestors are those people who went before us.]

an·nex (ə neks′ *for verb;* an′eks *for noun*), **1.** *v.* to join or add a smaller thing to a larger thing: *The United States annexed Texas in 1845.* **2.** *n.* something annexed; an added part, especially to a building: *We are building an annex to the school. n., pl.* **an·nex·es. –an′nex·a′tion,** *n.*

a·non·y·mous (ə non′ə məs), *adj.* **1.** by or from a person whose name is not known or given: *An anonymous letter is one which does not give the name of the writer.* **2.** unknown: *This book was written by an anonymous author.* **–a·non′y·mous·ly,** *adv.*

an·tag·o·nist (an tag′ə nist), *n.* person who fights, struggles, or contends against another in a combat or contest of any kind; adversary; opponent: *The knight defeated each antagonist who came against him.*

an·te·ced·ent (an′tə sēd′nt), **1.** *n.* the noun or noun phrase to which a pronoun refers. In "The dog which killed the rat is brown," *dog* is the antecedent of *which.* **2.** *adj.* coming or happening before; previous: *Cave dwellers lived in a period of history antecedent to written records.* **3.** *n.* a previous happening or event.

an·thro·pol·o·gist (an′thrə pol′ə jist), *n.* person who studies human beings, dealing especially with their fossil remains, physical characteristics, cultures, customs, and beliefs.

an·thro·pol·o·gy (an′thrə pol′ə jē), *n.* the science or study of human beings, dealing especially with their fossil remains, physical characteristics, cultures, customs, and beliefs. **–an′thro·po·log′i·cal,** *adj.* [**Anthropology** comes from the Greek words meaning "study of a human being."]

an·ti·bi·ot·ic (an′ti bī ot′ik), *n.* substance produced by a living thing, especially a bacterium or mold, that destroys or weakens germs. Penicillin is an antibiotic. Antibiotics are prescribed to treat bacterial infections.

an·ti·es·tab·lish·ment (an′tē e stab′lish mənt), *adj.* against the group that holds positions of influence or authority in a country, society, etc.; against the government.

an·ti·per·spir·ant (an′ti pėr′spər ənt), *n.* a chemical preparation that is applied to the skin to decrease perspiration and control body odor.

an·ti·so·cial (an′ti sō′shəl), *adj.* **1.** opposed to the principles upon which society is based: *Stealing is an antisocial act.* **2.** opposed to friendly relationship and normal companionship with others: *Hermits are antisocial.*

an·ti·war (an′tē wôr), *adj.* opposed to war.

a in *hat*	o in *hot*	ch in *child*
ā in *age*	ō in *open*	ng in *long*
â in *care*	ȯ in *all*	sh in *she*
ä in *far*	ô in *order*	th in *thin*
e in *let*	oi in *oil*	ŦH in *then*
ē in *equal*	ou in *out*	zh in *measure*
ėr in *term*	u in *cup*	ə = a in *about*
i in *it*	ů in *put*	ə = e in *taken*
ī in *ice*	ü in *rule*	ə = i in *pencil*

anx·ious·ly (angk′shəs lē *or* ang′shəs lē), *adv.* **1.** with uneasiness because of thoughts or fears of what may happen; with an uneasy feeling. **2.** with eager desire.

aph·o·rism (af′ə riz′əm), *n.* a short sentence expressing a general truth or some practical wisdom; maxim; proverb. EXAMPLE: "Live and let live."

a·rach·no·pho·bi·a (ə rak′nə fō′bē ə), *n.* abnormal fear of arachnids, such as spiders and scorpions.

ar·cha·ism (är′kē iz′əm), *n.* word or expression no longer in general use.

ar·chi·tect (är′kə tekt), *n.* **1.** person who designs and makes plans for buildings and sees that these plans are followed by the people who put up the buildings. **2.** maker; creator: *The architects of the United Nations hoped for lasting world peace.*

ar·dor (är′dər), *n.* great enthusiasm; eagerness; zeal: *The senator spoke with ardor about the need for gun control.*

ar·e·a (âr′ē ə), *n.* **1.** amount or extent of surface, especially the measure in square units: *The area of this floor is 600 square feet.* **2.** region or district: *The Rocky Mountain area is very scenic. n., pl.* **ar·e·as.**

ar·is·toc·ra·cy (ar′ə stok′rə sē), *n.* **1.** class of people having a high position in society because of birth, rank, or title; nobility. Earls, duchesses, etc., belong to the aristocracy. **2.** class of people considered superior because of intelligence, culture, or wealth; upper class. **3.** government in which the nobility or any privileged upper class rules. *n., pl.* **ar·is·toc·ra·cies.**

ar·thro·pod (är′thrə pod), *n.* any animal without a backbone having a jointed body and jointed legs. Insects, spiders, and lobsters are three kinds of arthropods. [**Arthropod** comes from Greek words meaning "jointed foot." In fact, however, it is the legs, not the feet, that are jointed.]

ar·ti·fact (är′tə fakt), *n.* anything made by human skill or work, especially a tool or weapon.

ar·ti·fi·cial (är′tə fish′əl), *adj.* **1.** made by human skill or labor; not natural: *Plastics are artificial substances that do not occur in nature.* **2.** made as a substitute or imitation; not real: *We made artificial paper flowers.* **–ar′ti·fi′cial·ly,** *adv.* **–art′ti·fi′cial·ness,** *n.*

as·so·ci·a·tion (ə sō′sē ā′shən *or* ə sō′shē ā′shən), *n.* **1.** group of people joined together for some purpose; society: *Will you join the young people's association at our church?* **2.** idea connected with another idea in thought: *Some people make the association of the color red with anger.*

as·sump·tion (ə sump′shən), *n.* **1.** thing assumed: *His assumption that he would win proved incorrect.* **2.** act of assuming: *The nation celebrated the new president's assumption of office.*

as·ter (as′tər), *n.* any of many common plants with daisylike flowers that have white, pink, or purple petals around a yellow center. **–as′ter·like′,** *adj.* [**Aster** comes from a Greek word meaning "star." The flower has a starlike appearance.]

as·ter·isk (as′tə risk′), *n.* a star-shaped mark (*) used in printing and writing to call attention to a footnote, indicate the omission of words or letters, etc. [**Asterisk** comes from a Greek word meaning "small star," which is just what it looks like.]

as·ter·oid (as′tə roid′), *n.* any of thousands of rocky objects smaller than 620 miles (1000 kilometers) across, orbiting the sun mainly between the orbits of Mars and Jupiter; planetoid.

as·tron·o·mer (ə stron′ə mər), *n.* an expert in astronomy.

as·tron·o·my (ə stron′ə mē), *n.* science that deals with the sun, moon, planets, stars, etc. It studies their motions, positions, distances, sizes, etc. [**Astronomy** comes from Greek words meaning "star" and "law."]

au·di·ble (ȯ′də bəl), *adj.* able to be heard; loud enough to be heard: *Without a microphone the speaker was barely audible.* **–au·di·bil·i·ty** (ȯ′də bil′ə tē), *n.* **–au′di·bly,** *adv.*

au·di·o·vis·u·al (ȯ′dē ō vizh′ü əl), *adj.* of hearing and sight. Schools use movies, slides, recordings, and other devices as audiovisual aids in teaching. **–au′di·o·vis′u·al·ly,** *adv.*

au·di·tion (ȯ dish′ən), **1.** *n.* act of hearing to test the ability, quality, or performance of a singer, actor, or other performer. **2.** *v.* to give a singer, actor, or other performer such a hearing. **3.** *v.* to sing, act, or perform at such a hearing.

au·di·to·ri·um (ȯ′də tôr′ē əm), *n.* **1.** large room for an audience in a church, theater, school, etc. **2.** a building especially designed for public meetings, concerts, lectures, etc. *n., pl.* **au·di·to·ri·ums, au·di·to·ri·a** (ȯ′də tôr′ē ə).

au·then·tic·i·ty (ȯ then tis′ə tē), *n.* **1.** reliability: *The value of the evidence depends on its authenticity.* **2.** genuineness: *The lawyer questioned the authenticity of the signature.*

au·to·crat·ic (ȯ′tə krat′ik), *adj.* of or like an autocrat; having absolute power or authority; ruling without checks or limitations: *The principal's autocratic manner made him unpopular.* **–au′to·crat′i·cal·ly,** *adv.*

au·ton·o·mous (ȯ ton′ə məs), *adj.* self-governing; independent: *an autonomous nation.* **–au·ton′o·mous·ly,** *adv.*

Bb

basin (bā′sn), *n.* **1.** a wide, shallow bowl for holding liquids. **2.** all the land drained by a river and the streams that flow into it: *The Mississippi basin extends from the Appalachians to the Rockies.* **–ba′sin·like′**, *adj.*

bat·ter·y (bat′ər ē), *n.* **1.** container holding materials that produce electricity by chemical action; a single electric cell: *Most flashlights work on two batteries.* **2.** any set of things similar or connected to each other: *a battery of microphones, a battery of tests. n., pl.* **bat·ter·ies.**

bel·low (bel′ō), **1.** *v.* to make a loud, deep noise; roar: *The bull bellowed.* **2.** *n.* a loud, deep noise; roar. **–bel′low·er**, *n.*

ben·e·fac·tor (ben′ə fak′tər), *n.* person who has given money or kindly help.

ben·e·fi·cial (ben′ə fish′əl), *adj.* producing good; favorable; helpful: *Daily exercise is beneficial to your health.* **–ben′e·fi′cial·ly**, *adv.* **–ben′e·fi′cial·ness**, *n.*

ben·e·fi·ci·ar·y (ben′ə fish′ē er′ē), *n.* **1.** person who receives benefit: *All the children are beneficiaries of the new playground.* **2.** person who receives money or property from an insurance policy, a will, etc. *n., pl.* **ben·e·fi·ci·ar·ies.**

be·nev·o·lent (bə nev′ə lənt), *adj.* having a desire to promote the happiness of others; kindly; charitable. **–be·nev′o·lent·ly**, *adv.*

bi·o·di·ver·si·ty (bī′ō di vėr′sə tē), *n.* a wide variety of different species living together in one place.

bi·og·ra·phy (bī og′rə fē), *n.* an account of someone's life. *n., pl.* **bi·og·ra·phies.**

bi·ol·o·gist (bī ol′ə jist), *n.* expert in the scientific study of living things.

bi·on·ic (bī on′ik), *adj.* **1.** of or about bionics, the study of the anatomy and physiology of animals as a basis for designing new or improved electronic devices or systems. **2.** having both biological and electronic parts.

bi·op·sy (bī′op sē), *n.* the removal of cells or tissue from a living body for medial examination. *n., pl.* **bi·op·sies.**

bi·o·tech·nol·o·gy (bī′ō tek nol′ə jē), *n.* the industrial use of living things, such as microorganisms, or other biological substances to manufacture products and carry out services. Biotechnology is used to manufacture drugs and to recycle waste.

bi·sect (bī′sekt), *v.* to divide into two equal parts: *You can bisect a 90-degree angle into two 45-degree angles.*

black hole, *n.* an astronomical object that is supposed to have been created by a collapsed star. Its mass is so great in proportion to its radius that its extreme gravity prevents even light from escaping.

block·ade (blo kād′), **1.** *n.* act of blocking a place by military means to control who or what goes into or out of it. **2.** *v.* to put under blockade. *v.* **block·ad·ed, block·ad·ing. –block·ad′er**, *n.*

bolt (bōlt), **1.** *n.* a metal rod with a head at one end and a screw thread for a nut at the other. Bolts are used to fasten things together or hold something in place. **2.** *v.* to dash off; run away: *The horse bolted at the sight of the car.*

buoy·ant (boi′ənt *or* bü′yənt), *adj.* **1.** tending to float: *Wood and cork are buoyant in water; iron and lead are not.* **2.** tendency to be cheerful and hopeful; lighthearted: *I was in a buoyant mood on that sunny morning.* **–buoy′ant·ly**, *adv.*

bur·eau·crat (byůr′ə krat), *n.* **1.** official in a bureaucracy. **2.** a government official who insists on a rigid routine. **–bur′eau·crat′ic**, *adj.* **–bur′eau·crat′i·cal·ly**, *adv.*

by·law (bī′lȯ′), *n.* law made by a city, company, club, etc., for the control of its own affairs.

Cc

can·did·ly (kan′did lē), *adv.* **1.** said openly; frankly; sincerely. **2.** fairly; impartially.

cap·il·lar·y (kap′ə ler′ē), *n.* a blood vessel with a very slender, hairlike opening. Capillaries join the end of an artery to the beginning of a vein. *n., pl.* **cap·il·lar·ies.**

car·di·ol·o·gist (kär′dē ol′ə jist), *n.* person who specializes in the branch of medicine that deals with the heart and the diagnosis and treatment of its diseases.

car·nage (kär′nij), *n.* slaughter of a great number of people or animals.

car·ni·val (kär′nə vəl), *n.* **1.** place of amusement or a traveling show having merry-go-rounds, games, sideshows, etc. **2.** feasting and merrymaking; noisy and unrestrained revels. [**Carnival** comes from an Italian word meaning "taking away meat." Traditionally, people ate no meat during Lent and celebrated carnival just before Lent.]

car·niv·or·ous (kär niv′ər əs), *adj.* feeding chiefly on flesh; meat-eating. Cats, dogs, lions, tigers, and sharks are carnivorous animals. **–car·niv′or·ous·ly**, *adv.* **–car·niv′or·ous·ness**, *n.*

car·tog·ra·phy (kär tog′rə fē), *n.* the making or study of maps or charts.

cen·sus (sen′səs), *n.* an official count of the people of a country or district. It is taken to find out the number of people, their age, sex, what they do to make a living, and many other facts about them. *n., pl.* **cen·sus·es.**

cen·ti·pede (sen′tə pēd′), *n.* any of many flat, wormlike animals with many pairs of legs, the front pair of which are claw-like and contain poison glands.

cen·trip·e·tal (sen trip′ə təl), *adj.* moving toward the center. **–cen·trip′e·tal·ly,** *adv.*

cir·cuit (sėr′kit), *n.* **1.** act of going around: *It takes a year for Earth to make its circuit of the sun.* **2.** the complete path over which an electric current flows.

cir·cum·nav·i·gate (sėr′kəm nav′ə gāt), *v.* to sail around; *Magellan's ship circumnavigated Earth.* *v.* **cir·cum·nav·i·gat·ed, cir·cum·nav·i·gat·ing. –cir′cum·nav′i·ga′tion,** *n.*

cir·cum·spect (sėr′kəm spekt), *adj.* watchful on all sides; careful; cautious; prudent: *circumspect actions.* **–cir′cum·spect′ly,** *adv.* **–cir′cum·spect′ness,** *n.*

cir·cum·stance (sėr′kəm stans), *n.* **1.** condition that accompanies an act or event: *Unfavorable circumstances such as fog and rain often delayed us on our trip to the mountains.* **2.** fact or event: *It was a lucky circumstance that I found my money.*

cir·cum·vent (sėr′kəm vent′), *v.* **1.** to get the better of or defeat by trickery; outwit: *The dishonest official was always trying to circumvent the law.* **2.** to go around: *He took a roundabout route to circumvent the traffic.* **–cir′cum·ven′tion,** *n.*

cit·i·zen (sit′ə zən), *n.* **1.** person who by birth or by choice is a member of a nation. A citizen owes loyalty to that nation and is given certain rights by it. *Many immigrants have become citizens of the United States.* **2.** inhabitant of a city or town.

civ·ics (siv′iks), *n.* study of the duties, rights, and privileges of citizens.

civ·il (siv′əl), *adj.* **1.** of a citizen or citizens: *Voting and paying taxes are civil duties.* **2.** of the government, state, or nation: *Police departments are civil institutions to protect local citizens.*

ci·vil·i·ty (sə vil′ə tē), *n.* **1.** polite behavior; courtesy: *Thank you for your civility in replying to my letter so promptly.* **2.** act or expression of politeness or courtesy. *n., pl.* **ci·vil·i·ties** for 2.

civ·i·li·za·tion (siv′ə lə zā′shən), *n.* **1.** nations and peoples that have reached advanced stages in social development: *All civilization should be aroused against war.* **2.** the ways of living of a people or nation: *The civilizations of ancient Egypt and ancient Greece had many contacts over the centuries.*

claim·ant (klā′mənt), *n.* person who makes a claim.

clam·or (klam′ər), **1.** *n.* a loud noise, especially of voices; continual uproar: *The clamor of the crowd filled the air.* **2.** *v.* to make a loud noise or continual uproar; shout.

clause (klȯz), *n.* **1.** part of a sentence having a subject and predicate. In "He came before we left," "He came" is a main clause that can stand alone as a sentence, and "before we left" is a subordinate clause that depends upon the main clause for completion of its meaning. **2.** a single paragraph or division of a contract, deed, will, or any other written agreement: *A clause in our lease says we may not keep a dog in this building.*

claus·tro·pho·bi·a (klȯ′strə fō′bē ə), *n.* an abnormal fear or enclosed spaces: *Elevators give me claustrophobia.*

clear·ance (klir′əns), *n.* **1.** act of clearing away anything no longer wanted where it is: *slum clearance.* **2.** sale of goods at reduced prices.

cli·ché (klē shā′), *n.* expression or idea worn out by long use. *n., pl.* **cli·chés.** [**Cliché** comes from a French word meaning "a block of printing type." Once type had been formed into a block, it could be used over and over by a newspaper or magazine, until it wore out from long use.]

co·au·thor (kō ȯ′thər), *n.* a joint author.

co·ed·u·ca·tion·al (kō′ej ə kā′shə nəl), *adj.* educating boys and girls or men and women together in the same school or classes. **–co′ed·u·ca′tion·al·ly,** *adv.*

co·ef·fi·cient (kō′ə fish′ənt), *n.* number or symbol put with and multiplying another. In "3*x*," "3" is the coefficient of "*x*," and "*x*" is the coefficient of "3."

co·ex·ist (kō′ig zist′), *v.* **1.** to exist together or at the same time. **2.** to live in peace with others in spite of differences: *Our cats and dogs coexist happily.*

cog·i·tate (koj′ə tāt), *v.* to think over; consider with care; ponder; meditate: *The judge cogitated a long time before making any decision.* *v.* **cog·i·tat·ed, cog·i·tat·ing. –cog′i·ta′tion,** *n.*

co·in·ci·dence (kō in′sə dəns), *n.* **1.** the happening by chance of two things at the same time or place in such a way as to seem remarkable or planned: *It is a coincidence that my cousin and I were born on the very same day.* **2.** act of coinciding: *the coincidence of two triangles.*

col·o·nize (kol′ə nīz), *v.* to establish a colony or colonies in: *The English colonized New England.* *v.* **col·o·nized, col·o·niz·ing, –col′o·ni·za′tion,** *n.* **–col′o·niz′er,** *n.*

com·mem·o·rate (kə mem′ə rāt′), *v.* to honor the memory of; *a stamp commemorating the landing of the Pilgrims.* *v.* **com·mem·o·rat·ed, com·mem·o·rat·ing, –com·mem′o·ra′tor,** *n.*

com·merce (kom′ərs), *n.* the buying and selling of goods, especially in large amounts between different places; business; trade.

com·mune (kom′yün), *n.* **1.** the smallest division for local government in France, Belgium, and several other European countries. **2.** group of people living together.

com·mu·nism (kom′yə niz′əm), *n.* **1.** an economic and social system in which most or all property is owned by the state or community as a whole and is shared by all. **2. Communism,** the principles and practices of members of a Communist party.

com·pe·ti·tion (kom′pə tish′ən), *n.* **1.** act of trying hard to win or gain something wanted by others; rivalry: *competition among stores for customers.* **2.** contest: *She won first place in the swimming competition.*

complex fraction, *n.* fraction having a fraction in the numerator, in the denominator, or in both; compound fraction.
EXAMPLES: $\frac{1\frac{3}{4}}{3}, \frac{1}{3\frac{3}{4}}, \frac{\frac{3}{4}}{1\frac{7}{8}}$.

com·po·nent (kəm pō′nənt), **1.** *n.* a necessary or essential part: *Quartz and feldspar are the chief components of granite.* **2.** *adj.* forming a necessary part; making up; constituent: *component parts.*

compound interest, *n.* interest paid on both the original sum of money borrowed or invested and the interest added to it.

con·cede (kən sēd′), *v.* **1.** to admit as true; acknowledge: *The candidate conceded defeat in the election.* **2.** to allow someone to have; grant: *They conceded us the right to use their driveway.* *v.* **con·ced·ed, con·ced·ing, –con·ced′er,** *n.*

con·clu·sion (kən klü′zhən), *n.* **1.** final part; end: *The end of each chapter in our science book has a conclusion summing up all the important facts.* **2.** a final result; outcome: *bring work to a good conclusion.*

con·du·cive (kən dü′siv), *adj.* favorable; helpful: *Exercise is conducive to good health.* **–con·du′cive·ness,** *n.*

con·fec·tion·er·y (kən fek′shə ner′ē), *n.* **1.** candies or sweets; confections. **2.** place where confections, ice cream, and cakes are made or sold. *n., pl.* **con·fec·tion·er·ies** for 2.

con·fed·e·ra·tion (kən fed′ə rā′shən), *n.* league; confederacy; alliance: *The United States was originally a confederation of 13 colonies.*

con·gen·ial (kə jē′nyəl), *adj.* **1.** having similar tastes and interests; getting on well together: *Congenial companions made the trip pleasant.* **2.** agreeable; suitable: *The young scientist found laboratory work more congenial than teaching science.* **–con·gen′ial·ly,** *adv.*

Con·gress (kong′gris), *n.* the national lawmaking group of the United States, consisting of the Senate and the House of Representatives, with members elected from every state.

con·gru·ent (kən grü′ənt *or* kong′grü ənt), *adj.* exactly coinciding: *Congruent triangles have the same size and shape.* **–con·gru′ent·ly,** *adv.*

con·sen·sus (kən sen′səs), *n.* general agreement; opinion of all or most of the people consulted: *After much debate, the club members reached a consensus about adopting the proposal.* *n., pl.* **con·sen·sus·es.**

con·ser·va·to·ry (kən sėr′və tôr′ē), *n.* **1.** school for instruction in music. **2.** greenhouse for growing and displaying plants and flowers. *n., pl.* **con·serv·a·to·ries.**

con·spic·u·ous (kən spik′yü əs), *adj.* **1.** easily seen: *A traffic light should be placed where it is conspicuous.* **2.** attracting notice; remarkable: *conspicuous bravery.* **–con·spic′u·ous·ly,** *adv.* **–con·spic′u·ous·ness,** *n.*

con·sum·er (kən sü′mər), *n.* **1.** person who buys and uses food, clothing, or anything grown or made by producers: *A low price for wheat should reduce the price of flour to the consumer.* **2.** any living thing that has to eat in order to stay alive. Animals are consumers, but plants make their own food.

con·tem·plate (kon′təm plāt), *v.* **1.** to look at or think about for a long time; study carefully: *We contemplated the beautiful mountain landscape.* **2.** to have in mind; consider, intend, or inspect: *She is contemplating a trip to Europe.* *v.* **con·tem·plat·ed, con·tem·plat·ing. –con′tem·pla′tor,** *n.*

con·tract (kən trakt′ *for 1;* kon′trakt *for 2*), **1.** *v.* to draw together; make shorter: *The earthworm contracted its body.* **2.** *n.* a written agreement that can be enforced by law.

con·tra·dict (kon′trə dikt′), *v.* **1.** to say that a statement is not true; deny: *The company contradicts the government report and says it does not pollute the river.* **2.** to be opposite to; disagree with: *Your story and her story contradict each other.* **–con′tra·dict′a·ble,** *adj.* **–con′tra·dic′tor,** *n.*

con·ver·sion (kən vėr′zhən), *n.* **1.** act or process of changing or turning; change: *Heat causes the conversion of water into steam.* **2.** a change from unbelief to faith; change from one religion, party, etc., to another.

con·vert (kən vėrt′), *v.* **1.** to turn to another or a particular use or purpose; change: *The generators at the dam convert water power into electricity.* **2.** to exchange for an equivalent: *She converted her dollars into pounds upon arriving in London.*

con·vo·lut·ed (kon′və lü′tid), *adj.* **1.** complicated; intricate: *a convoluted story.* **2.** tangled; winding: *a convoluted vine.*

cop·y·right (kop′ē rīt′), **1.** *n.* the exclusive right to publish or sell a certain book, picture, etc., granted by a government for a certain number of years. **2.** *v.* to protect by getting a copyright. Books, pieces of music, plays, software, etc., are usually copyrighted.

correction|degradation

cor·rec·tion (kə rek′shən), *n.* **1.** a change to correct an error or mistake: *Write in your corrections neatly.* **2.** act of correcting; setting right: *The correction of all my mistakes took nearly an hour.* **–cor·rec′tion·al,** *adj.*

cor·rel·a·tive (kə rel′ə tiv), **1.** *adj.* having a mutual relation. Conjunctions used in pairs, such as *either... or,* are correlative. **2.** *n.* either of two things having a mutual relation and commonly used together. Pairs of words like *husband* and *wife, mother* and *father,* are correlatives. **–cor·rel′a·tive·ly,** *adv.*

cos·mic (koz′mik), *adj.* **1.** having to do with the whole universe: *Cosmic forces produce galaxies.* **2.** vast: *the cosmic amounts of money spent each day.* **–cos′mi·cal·ly,** *adv.*

cos·mo·naut (koz′mə nôt), *n.* a Soviet astronaut.

cos·mo·pol·i·tan (koz′mə pol′ə tən), **1.** *adj.* free from national or local prejudices; feeling at home in all parts of the world: *Diplomats are usually cosmopolitan people.* **2.** *n.* person who feels at home in all parts of the world.

coup (kü), *n.* **1.** a sudden, brilliant action; unexpected, clever move; master stroke. **2.** coup d'état. *n., pl.* **coups** (küz).

co·work·er (kō′wėr′kər), *n.* person who works with another.

cra·ni·um (krā′nē əm), *n.* **1.** the skull of any animal that has a backbone. **2.** the part of the skull that encloses the brain. *n., pl.* **cra·ni·ums, cra·ni·a** (krā′nē ə).

cred·i·bil·i·ty (kred′ə bil′ə tē), *n.* fact or quality of being worthy of belief or reliable.

cri·ter·i·a (krī tir′ē ə), *n.* rules or standards for making a judgment; test.

crit·i·cal (krit′ə kəl), *adj.* **1.** inclined to find fault or disapprove: *a critical disposition.* **2.** coming from someone who is skilled as a critic: *a critical judgment, critical essays.* **–crit′i·cal·ly,** *adv.* **–crit′i·cal·ness,** *n.*

crit·i·cism (krit′ə siz′əm), *n.* **1.** unfavorable remarks or judgments; finding fault: *I could not let their rudeness pass without criticism.* **2.** act of making judgments; analysis of merits and faults: *literary criticism, drama criticism.*

cross-ref·er·ence (krôs′ref′ər əns), *n.* reference from one part of a book, index, etc., to another.

cube (kyüb), **1.** *n.* a solid object with six square faces or sides, all equal. **2.** *v.* to use a number three times as a factor: *5 cubed is 125, because 5 x 5 x 5 = 125.* **3.** *n.* product obtained when a number is cubed: *The cube of 4 is 64.* *v.* **cubed, cub·ing. –cube′like′,** *adj.*

cu·bic (kyü′bik), *adj.* **1.** shaped like a cube: *the cubic form of a block of ice.* **2.** of or for cubic measure. A cubic foot is the volume of a cube with edges that are each one foot long. Any other cubic unit is the volume of a cube with each side of the length named.

cur·rent (kėr′ənt), *n.* **1.** a flow of water, air, or any fluid; running stream: *The current swept the stick down the river.* **2.** flow of electricity through a wire or other conductor: *The current failed when wind knocked down the power lines.*

curt·ly (kėrt′lē), *adv.* rudely; abruptly.

cyl·in·der (sil′ən dər), *n.* **1.** any long, round object, solid, or hollow, with flat ends. Rollers and tin cans are cylinders. **2.** a solid bounded by two equal, parallel circles and by a curved surface, formed by moving a straight line of fixed length so that its ends always lie on the two parallel circles. [**Cylinder** comes from a Greek word meaning "to roll." In ancient times, the only way to move heavy objects such as building stones was on rollers, usually wooden ones. Anything shaped like a round log was called a roller too.]

Dd

de·cep·tion (di sep′shən), *n.* **1.** act of misleading; deceiving: *The twins' deception in exchanging places fooled everybody except their parents.* **2.** trick meant to deceive; fraud; sham: *The scheme is all a deception to cheat people out of their money.*

de·claim (di klām′), *v.* **1.** to recite in public; make a formal speech. **2.** to speak like an orator in a loud and emotional manner; speak for effect: *The politician declaimed against the opposing party.* **–de·claim′er,** *n.*

de·clar·a·tive (di klar′ə tiv), *adj.* making a statement; explaining. "I'm eating" and "The dog has four legs" are declarative sentences.

de·duce (di düs′), *v.* to reach a conclusion by reasoning; infer: *I deduced from your lack of appetite what had happened to the cookies.* *v.* **de·duced, de·duc·ing. –de·duc′i·ble,** *adj.*

de·duc·tion (di duk′shən), *n.* **1.** act or process of taking away; subtraction: *No deduction from your pay was made for absence due to illness.* **2.** act or process of reaching conclusions by reasoning; inference.

de·fi·cit (def′ə sit), *n.* amount by which a sum of money falls short; shortage: *Since the club owed $15 and had only $10 in the treasury, there was a deficit of $5 to be made up by the members.*

deg·ra·da·tion (deg′rə dā′shən), *n.* **1.** act or process of degrading: *A poor diet may cause a gradual degradation of health.* **2.** condition of being degraded: *an environment's degradation by pollution.*

de·hy·drate (dē hī′drāt), *v.* **1.** to take water or moisture from; dry: *to dehydrate vegetables. High fever dehydrates the body.* **2.** to lose water or moisture. *v.* **de·hy·drat·ed, de·hy·drat·ing. –de′hy·dra′tion,** *n.* **–de·hy′dra·tor,** *n.*

de·mise (di mīz′), *n.* death.

de·mol·ish (di mol′ish), *v.* **1.** to pull or tear down; destroy: *The old building was demolished to make room for a new one.* **2.** to put an end to; ruin completely: *Their scorn demolished my self-satisfaction.* **–de·mol′ish·er,** *n.*

de·nom·i·na·tion (di nom′ə nā′shən), *n.* **1.** name for a group or class of things; name. **2.** a religious group or sect: *Methodists and Baptists are two large Protestant denominations.*

de·no·ta·tion (dē′nō tā′shən), *n.* **1.** meaning, especially the exact, literal meaning. The denotation of *home* is "place where you live," but it has many connotations. **2.** act of denoting or marking out; indication.

de·noue·ment (dā′nü män′), *n.* solution of a plot in a story, play, situation, etc.; outcome; end.

den·tist (den′tist), *n.* doctor whose work is the care of teeth. A dentist fills cavities in teeth, cleans, straightens, or pulls them, and supplies caps, crowns, or artificial teeth.

de·plete (di plēt′), *v.* to reduce the amount of; empty; exhaust: *Rapid consumption of our resources can quickly deplete them. v.* **de·plet·ed, de·plet·ing. –de·ple′tion,** *n.*

de·port (di pôrt′), *v.* **1.** to force to leave; banish; expel. Deported aliens are sent out of the country, usually back to their native lands. **2.** to behave or conduct yourself in a particular manner: *The children deport themselves well when we have guests.* **–de·port′a·ble,** *adj.*

de·scrip·tion (di skrip′shən), *n.* **1.** composition or account that describes or gives a picture in words: *The reporter's vivid description of the hotel fire made me feel as if I were right at the scene.* **2.** act of telling or writing how someone looks, feels, or acts or how a place, thing, or event looks.

des·pot (des′pət), *n.* **1.** monarch having unlimited power; absolute ruler. **2.** person who does just as he or she likes; tyrant.

de·ter·mine (di tėr′mən), *v.* **1.** to make up your mind very firmly; resolve: *He determined to become the best player on the team.* **2.** to find out exactly: *The pilot determined how far she was from the airport. v.* **de·ter·mined, de·ter·min·ing.**

de·volve (di volv′), *v.* **1.** to be handed down to someone else; be transferred: *When she resigned as president, her duties devolved upon the vice-president.* **2.** to transfer duty, work, etc., to someone else. **3.** to deteriorate gradually. *v.* **de·volved, de·volv·ing. –de·volve′ment,** *n.*

di·a·lect (dī′ə lekt), *n.* a form of speech spoken in a certain district or by a certain group of people: *The Scottish dialect of English has many words and pronunciations that Americans do not use.*

dic·tate (dik′tāt), *v.* **1.** to say or read aloud for another person to write down, or for a machine to record: *The teacher dictated a list of books to the students. She dictates letters to her secretary each morning.* **2.** to speak with authority; give a direction or order that must be carried out or obeyed: *The country that won the war dictated the terms of peace to the country that lost.* *v.* **dic·tat·ed, dic·tat·ing.**

dic·ta·tor (dik′tā tər), *n.* **1.** person who uses absolute authority: *The dictator seized control of the government and took complete power over the people of the country.* **2.** person who says or reads something aloud for another to write down.

dic·tion (dik′shən), *n.* **1.** manner of expressing ideas in words; style of speaking or writing. Good diction involves using words accurately as a speaker or a writer to express your ideas. **2.** manner of pronouncing words; enunciation.

dif·fe·ren·ti·ate (dif′ə ren′shē āt), *v.* **1.** to make different; cause to have differences: *Consideration for others differentiates a thoughtful person from a thoughtless one.* **2.** to tell the difference in or between; find or show to be different: *Some color-blind people cannot differentiate red from green. v.* **dif·fe·ren·ti·at·ed, dif·fe·ren·ti·at·ing. –dif′fe·ren′ti·a′tion,** *n.*

dif·frac·tion (di frak′shən), *n.* **1.** process of the spreading of light around an obstacle into a series of light and dark bands or into the colored bands of the spectrum. **2.** a similar process of the spreading of sound waves, radio waves, etc.

dif·fu·sion (di fyü′zhən), *n.* **1.** act or process of spreading or scattering widely: *The invention of printing greatly increased the diffusion of knowledge.* **2.** condition of being widely spread or scattered.

di·men·sion (də men′shən), *n.* **1.** measurement of length, breadth, or thickness: *I need wallpaper for a room of the following dimensions: 16 feet long, 12 feet wide, 9 feet high.* **2.** Also, **dimensions,** *pl.* size, extent: *Building a park in the slum area was a project of large dimensions.*

dip·lo·mat (dip′lə mat), *n.* **1.** person whose work is to manage the relations between his or her nation and other nations. **2.** person who is skillful in dealing with others; tactful person.

di·rec·tor (də rek′tər *or* dī rek′tər), *n.* **1.** person who directs; manager. A person who directs the performance of a play, a movie, or a TV or radio show is called a director. **2.** one of a group of people who direct the affairs of a company or institution.

dis·as·ter (də zas′tər), *n.* event that causes much suffering or loss; great misfortune such as a destructive fire or an earthquake. [**Disaster** comes from a French word meaning "unfavorable star." Long ago, many people believed that bad events were caused by unfavorable positions of the stars and planets.]

dis·pos·a·ble (dis pō′zə bəl), *adj.* able to be disposed of or thrown away after use: *disposable paper napkins.*

dis·pute (dis pyüt′), **1.** *v.* to give reasons or facts for or against something; argue; debate; discuss: *Congress disputed over the need for new taxes.* **2.** *n.* argument; debate: *There is a dispute over where to build the new school.* *v.* **dis·put·ed, dis·put·ing. –dis·put′er,** *n.*

dis·tract (dis trakt′), *v.* **1.** to draw away the mind, attention, etc.: *Noise distracts me when I am trying to study.* **2.** to confuse; disturb: *Several people talking at once distract a listener.*

dis·turb·ance (dis tėr′bəns), *n.* **1.** confusion; disorder: *The police were called to quiet the disturbance at the street corner.* **2.** uneasiness; trouble; worry.

di·ver·sion (də vėr′zhən), *n.* **1.** act of turning aside; a diverting: *A magician's talk creates a diversion of attention so that people do not see how the tricks are done.* **2.** distraction from work, care, etc.: amusement; entertainment; pastime: *Golf is my parents' favorite diversion.*

di·vert (də vėrt′), *v.* **1.** to turn aside: *A ditch diverted water from the stream into the fields. The siren of the fire engine diverted the audience's attention from the play.* **2.** to amuse; entertain: *Listening to music diverted him after a hard day's work.*

di·vi·sor (də vī′zər), *n.* number or quantity by which another is to be divided: *In 728 ÷ 16, 16 is the divisor.*

doc·u·ment (dok′yə mənt *for noun;* dok′yə ment *for verb*), **1.** *n.* something written or printed that gives information or proof of some fact; any object used as evidence. Letters, maps, and pictures are documents. **2.** *v.* to prove or support by means of documents or the like: *Can you document your theory with facts?*

dor·mi·to·ry (dôr′mə tôr′ē), *n.* **1.** a building with many rooms for sleeping in. Many colleges have dormitories for students whose homes are elsewhere. **2.** room for sleeping that has several beds. *n., pl.* **dor·mi·to·ries.**

dou·ble·speak (dub′əl spēk′), *n.* the use of indirect or complex language, often to conceal an unpleasant truth or mislead others. Referring to a fight as a "conflict situation" is an example of doublespeak.

down·grade (doun′grād′), **1.** *n.* a downward slope. **2.** *v.* to lower in position, importance, reputation, etc.: *downgrade an employee. He downgrades people he does not like, in spite of their merits.* *v.* **down·grad·ed, down·grad·ing.**

Ee

e·co·nom·ic (ē′kə nom′ik *or* ek′ə nom′ik), *adj.* **1.** of or about economics. Economic issues have to do with the production, distribution, and consumption of goods and services. **2.** of or about the management of the income, supplies, and expenses of a household, government, etc.

ed·i·to·ri·al (ed′ə tôr′ē əl), **1.** *n.* article in a newspaper or magazine giving the editor's or publisher's opinion on some subject: *Today's editorial was about gun control laws.* **2.** *adj.* of an editorial: *editorial work.* **–ed′i·to′ri·al·ly,** *adv.*

ed·u·cate (ej′ə kāt), *v.* **1.** to develop in knowledge or skill by teaching, training, or study; teach: *The job of teachers is to educate people.* **2.** to send to school: *My cousin is being educated in England.* *v.* **ed·u·cat·ed, ed·u·cat·ing. –ed′u·cat′a·ble,** *adj.*

ef·fi·cien·cy (ə fish′ən sē), *n.* **1.** ability to produce the effect wanted without a waste of time, energy, etc.: *The skilled carpenter worked with great efficiency.* **2.** efficient operation: *Argument reduces the efficiency of a committee.*

e·go·tist (ē′gə tist), *n.* **1.** person who thinks or talks about himself or herself too much; conceited person. **2.** a selfish person.

e·gress (ē′gres), *n.* **1.** a going out: *The door was locked and no other egress was possible.* **2.** a way out; exit; outlet: *The egress was plainly marked.* [**Egress** comes from a Latin word meaning "step out."]

e·lab·o·ra·tion (i lab′ə rā′shən), *n.* **1.** added details. **2.** something worked out with great care.

e·lec·tric·i·ty (i lek′tris′ə tē), *n.* **1.** form of energy that can produce light, heat, motion, and magnetic force. Electricity comes from generators for people to buy and use, but it can be produced in small amounts by running a comb through your hair or by chemical change in a flashlight battery. Most familiar forms of electricity involve the flow of electrons. **2.** electric current: *The storm damaged the wires carrying electricity to the house.* [**Electricity** comes from a Greek word meaning "amber." If amber is rubbed with a cloth, it becomes charged with electricity and attracts straws or hair. The ancient Greeks were the first to record this fact and give it a name.]

e·mer·gent (i mėr′jənt), *adj.* emerging.

em·i·grate (em′ə grāt), *v.* to leave your own country to settle in another: *My grandparents emigrated from Ireland to the United States.* *v.* **em·i·grat·ed, em·i·grat·ing.**

e·mis·sion (i mish′ən), *n.* **1.** act or fact of emitting; *the emission of light from the sun.* **2.** something emitted.

en·clave (en′klāv), *n.* country or district surrounded by territory of a foreign country: *Vatican City is an enclave in Rome, Italy.*

en·vi·ous (en′vē əs), *adj.* feeling or showing discontent because someone else has what you want; full of envy: *envious of another's good fortune.* **–en′vi·ous·ly,** *adv.* **–en′vi·ous·ness,** *n.*

en·zyme (en′zīm), *n.* any substance produced in living cells that influences a chemical reaction within a living thing without being changed itself. Some enzymes, such as pepsin, help break down food so that it can be digested.

e·quiv·a·lent (i kwiv′ə lənt), *adj.* **1.** equal; the same in value, effect, meaning, etc.: *Nodding is equivalent to saying yes.* **2.** (in mathematics) matching one-for-one, as some sets do. **–e·quiv′a·lent·ly,** *adv.*

e·quiv·o·cal (i kwiv′ə kəl), *adj.* **1.** having two or more meanings; ambiguous; *an equivocal answer.* **2.** undecided; uncertain: *Because so many voters are undecided, the result of the poll is equivocal.* **–e·quiv′o·cal·ly,** *adv.* **–e·quiv′o·cal·ness,** *n.*

e·rect (i rekt′), **1.** *adj.* straight up; not bending; not tipping; upright: *erect posture.* **2.** *v.* to put straight up; set upright: *They erected a TV antenna on the roof. The mast was erected on a firm base.* **e·rect′a·ble,** *adj.* **–e·rect′ly,** *adv.* **–e·rect′ness,** *n.* **–e·rect′or,** *n.*

es·ca·pade (es′kə pād), *n.* wild prank or adventure that breaks the rules.

es·ti·mate (es′tə mit *or* es′tə māt *for noun;* es′tə māt *for verb*) **1.** *n.* judgment or opinion about how much, how many, how good, etc.: *My estimate of the length of the room was 15 feet; it actually measured 14 feet, 9 inches.* **2.** *v.* to form a judgment or opinion about how much, how many, how good, etc.: *We estimated that it would take four hours to weed the garden.* *v.* **es·ti·mat·ed, es·ti·mat·ing. –es′ti·ma′tor,** *n.*

et·y·mol·o·gy (et′ə mol′ə jē), *n.* **1.** the history of a word. **2.** account or explanation of the origin and history of a word; word story. *n., pl.* **et·y·mol·o·gies. –et′y·mo·log′i·cal,** *adj.* **–et′y·mol′o·gist,** *n.*

eu·phe·mism (yü′fə miz′əm), *n.* a mild or indirect expression used instead of one that is harsh or unpleasantly direct. "Pass away" is a common euphemism for "die": "not very well" is a euphemism for "badly."

e·val·u·ate (i val′yü āt), *v.* to find out the value or the amount of; estimate the worth or importance of; appraise: *An expert will evaluate the paintings you wish to sell.* *v.* **e·val·u·at·ed, e·val·u·at·ing. –e·val′u·a′tor,** *n.*

e·vap·o·ra·tion (i vap′ə rā′shən), *n.* a changing of a liquid to a vapor.

e·vent (i vent′), *n.* **1.** a happening, especially an important happening: *Newspapers report current events.* **2.** one item in a program of sports: *The 100-yard dash was the last event.* [**Event** comes from a Latin word meaning "to come."]

ev·i·dence (ev′ə dəns), *n.* **1.** anything that shows what is true and what is not; facts; proof: *The evidence showed that he had not been there.* **2.** facts established and accepted in a court of law: *The judge heard all the evidence.*

ev·o·lu·tion (ev′ə lü′shən), *n.* **1.** a gradual development: *the evolution of transportation from horse and buggy to jet aircraft.* **2.** process in which slight bodily changes are passed from living things to their young, adding up to larger changes over a number of generations. According to Darwin's theory of evolution, all forms of life are the results of evolution from earlier forms, and the changes that adapt a living thing to its environment are the most likely to be passed on. [**Evolution** comes from Latin words meaning "to roll" and "out." The English word was originally used about movements of soldiers marching or riding horses, as they separated from each other and spread out over the land.]

ex·ceed (ek sēd′), *v.* **1.** to be more or greater than: *Lifting that heavy trunk exceeds my strength.* **2.** to do more than; go beyond: *Drivers are not supposed to exceed the speed limit.*

ex·claim (ek sklām′), *v.* to speak suddenly in surprise or strong feeling; cry out: *"That's wonderful!" she exclaimed.* **–ex·claim′er,** *n.*

ex·cla·ma·tion (ek′sklə mā′shən), *n.* something said suddenly as the result of surprise or strong feeling.

ex·clam·a·to·ry (ek sklam′ə tôr′ē), *adj.* using, containing, or expressing exclamation.

ex·clu·sion (ek sklü′zhən), *n.* act of excluding or condition of being excluded: *exclusion of trucks from one-way streets.*

ex·cre·tion (ek skrē′shən), *n.* **1.** a discharge of waste matter from the body. **2.** the waste matter that is separated and discharged.

ex·ile (eg′zīl *or* ek′sīl), **1.** *v.* to force to leave your country or home, often by law as a punishment; banish: *Napoleon was exiled to Elba.* **2.** *n.* condition of being exiled; banishment: *be sent into exile for life.* *v.* **ex·iled, ex·il·ing.**

ex·per·i·men·tal (ek sper′ə men′tl), *adj.* **1.** based on experiments: *Chemistry is an experimental science.* **2.** for testing or trying out: *The young bird made experimental attempts to fly.* **–exper′i·men′tal·ly,** *adv.*

ex·po·nent (ek spō′nənt), *n.* **1.** someone or something that explains. **2.** someone or something that stands as an example, type, or symbol of something: *Martin Luther King was a famous exponent of civil rights.*

ex·pose (ek spōz′), *v.* **1.** to lay open; leave without protection; uncover: *We were exposed to the hot sun all day while fishing. All the children have been exposed to mumps.* **2.** to make known; reveal: *She exposed the plot to the police. v.* **ex·posed, ex·pos·ing. –ex·pos′er,** *n.*

ex·po·si·tion (ek′spə zish′ən), *n.* **1.** a public show or exhibition; expo. A world's fair with exhibits from many countries is an exposition. **2.** speech or writing explaining a process, thing, or idea.

ex·ten·sion (ek sten′shən), *n.* **1.** act of extending: *the extension of a vacation for three more days, the extension of a road.* **2.** an extended part; addition: *The new extension to our school will make room for more students.*

ex·ter·mi·nate (ek stėr′mə nāt), *v.* to get rid of; destroy completely; kill: *This poison will exterminate rats. v.* **ex·ter·mi·nat·ed, ex·ter·mi·nat·ing. –ex·ter′mi·na′tion,** *n.*

Ff

fac·sim·i·le (fak sim′ə lē), *n.* **1.** an exact copy or likeness. **2.** fax.

fac·tion (fak′shən), *n.* group of persons who stand up for their side or act together for some common purpose against the rest of a larger group: *A faction in our club tried to make the president resign.* **–fac′tion·al,** *adj.*

false·hood (fòls′hu̇d), *n.* **1.** a false statement; lie. **2.** quality of being false.

fal·si·fy (fòl′sə fī), *v.* to make false; change in order to deceive; misrepresent: *He falsified his tax records. v.* **fal·si·fied, fal·si·fy·ing. –fal′si·fi′a·ble,** *adj.* **–fal·si·fi·ca′tion,** *n.* **–fal′si·fi′er,** *n.*

fan·ta·sy (fan′tə sē), *n.* **1.** creation or work of the imagination. Many stories, such as *Gulliver's Travels* and *Alice in Wonderland,* are fantasies. **2.** picture existing only in the mind; mental image or illusion; daydream: *I have a fantasy in which I win a million dollars. n., pl.* **fan·ta·sies.**

fascism (fash′iz′əm), *n.* **1.** the form of government in Italy from 1922 to 1943, under Benito Mussolini. **2.** the principles or methods of this or any similar government, or of a political party favoring such a government. Under fascism, a country is ruled by a dictator, with strong control of industry and labor by the central government, great restrictions upon the freedom of individuals, and extreme nationalism and militarism. [**Fascism** comes from a Latin word meaning "bundle." A bundle of sticks tied around an ax was a symbol of authority in ancient Rome. Italian dictator Benito Mussolini began using this symbol in 1919. You may find pictures of the Roman symbol on public buildings and monuments or even on old U.S. dimes.]

fer·ti·liz·er (fėr′tl ī′zer), *n.* substance such as manure, chemicals, etc., spread over or put into the soil to make it able to produce more.

fie·ry (fī′rē), *adj.* **1.** containing fire; burning; flaming: *a fiery furnace.* **2.** full of feeling or spirit: *a fiery speech. adj.* **fie·ri·er, fie·ri·est. –fi′er·i·ness,** *n.*

fig·ur·a·tive (fig′yər ə tiv), *adj.* **1.** using words out of their literal or ordinary meaning to add beauty or force. **2.** having many figures of speech. Much poetry is figurative. **–fig′ur·a·tive·ly,** *adv.* **–fig′ur·a·tive·ness,** *n.*

flus·tered (flus′tərd) *adj.* nervous and excited; confused.

fore·shad·ow (fôr shad′ō), *v.* to indicate beforehand; be a warning of: *Those clouds foreshadow a storm.* **–fore·shad′ow·er,** *n.*

frac·tion (frak′shən), *n.* **1.** one or more of the equal parts of a whole. $\frac{1}{2}$, $\frac{1}{3}$, and $\frac{3}{4}$ are fractions. **2.** a very small part, amount, etc.; not all of a thing; fragment: *She has done only a fraction of her homework.* [**Fraction** comes from a Latin word meaning "to break." A fraction is like a part broken off a larger number.]

fran·ti·cal·ly (fran′tik lē), *adv.* excitedly; wildly with rage, fear, pain, or grief.

fu·tu·ris·tic (fyü′chə ris′tik), *adj.* of or like the future; not traditional: *futuristic car design.*

Gg

gal·ax·y (gal′ək sē), *n.* **1.** group of billions of stars forming one system. Earth and the sun are in the Milky Way galaxy. Many galaxies outside our own can be seen with a telescope. **2.** a brilliant or splendid group, especially of very attractive or distinguished persons. *n., pl.* **gal·ax·ies.** [**Galaxy** comes from a Greek word meaning "milk." From Earth, the Milky Way looks like a streak of milk on the night sky.]

ge·net·ic (jə net′ik), *adj.* **1.** of or about a gene or genes: *a genetic mutation.* **2.** of genetics. **–ge·net′i·cal·ly,** *adv.*

ge·o·des·ic (jē′ə des′ik), *adj.* **1.** having to do with the part of mathematics that deals with the measurement of Earth and its gravity and with the location of points on Earth's surface. **2.** having a curve like the curvature of Earth.

ge·ol·o·gist (jē ol′ə jist), *n.* person who studies the composition of Earth or of other solid heavenly bodies, the processes that have formed them, and their history.

ge·ol·o·gy (jē ol′ə jē), *n.* **1.** science that deals with the composition of Earth or of other solid heavenly bodies, the processes that have formed them, and their history. **2.** physical features of an area of Earth or of a solid heavenly body; rocks, rock formation, etc., of a particular area.

ge·o·met·ric (jē ə met′rik), *adj.* **1.** of geometry; according to the principles of geometry: *geometric proof.* **2.** consisting of straight lines, circles, triangles, etc.; regular and symmetrical. **–ge′o·met′ri·cal·ly,** *adv.*

ge·o·po·lit·i·cal (jē′ō pə lit′ə kəl), *adj.* of the study of government and its policies as affected by physical geography.

gra·da·tion (grā dā′shən), *n.* **1.** one of the steps in a series: *the gradations of color in a rainbow.* **2.** a change by steps or stages; gradual change: *A camera lens allows gradation of the light that reaches the film.*

gra·di·ent (grā′dē ənt), *n.* **1.** rate of upward or downward slope of a road, railroad track, etc.: *steep gradients.* **2.** the sloping part of a road, railroad, etc.; grade.

grad·u·al (graj′ü əl), *adj.* happening slowly by small steps or degrees; changing step by step; moving little by little: *This low hill has a gradual slope. A child's growth into an adult is gradual.* **–grad′u·al·ly,** *adv.* **–grad′u·al·ness,** *n.*

gram·mar (gram′ər), *n.* **1.** the study of the forms and uses of words in sentences in a particular language. **2.** rules describing the use of words in a language.

graph·ic (graf′ik), *adj.* **1.** producing by words the effect of a picture; lifelike; vivid: *Her graphic description of the English countryside made me feel as though I had been there myself.* **2.** shown by a graph: *The school board kept a graphic record of school attendance for a month.* **–graph′i·cal·ly,** *adv.*

Hh

has·ten (hā′sn), *v.* **1.** to be quick; go fast: *She hastened to explain that she had not meant to be rude.* **2.** to cause to be quick; speed; hurry: *Sunshine and rest hastened his recovery.* **–hast′en·er,** *n.*

hex·a·gon (hek′sə gon), *n.* a plane figure having six angles and six sides.

hi·e·rar·chy (hī′ə rär′kē), *n.* **1.** organization of persons or things arranged one above the other according to rank, class, or grade. **2.** group of church officials of different ranks. The church hierarchy is composed of archbishops, bishops, priests, etc. *n., pl.* **hi·e·rar·chies.**

his·to·gram (his′te gram), *n.* a bar graph used to show the frequency of items in a set of data. Items are divided into as many groups as there are bars, and the height of each bar shows how many items are in that group.

his·to·ric (hi stôr′ik), *adj.* **1.** famous or important in history: *Plymouth Rock and Bunker Hill are historic spots.* **2.** of or about history.

hom·o·phone (hom′ə fōn), *n.* word having the same pronunciation as another, but a different spelling, origin, and meaning. *Ate* and *eight* are homophones.

hor·mone (hôr′mōn), *n.* any substance produced in one part of an animal or plant but controlling the activity of another part. In human beings, most hormones are formed in the endocrine glands and move through the bloodstream. Adrenalin and insulin are hormones. **–hor·mo′nal,** *adj.*

hy·per·ven·ti·late (hī′pər ven′tl āt), *v.* to breathe in too much air or too often, as when anxious or excited. This lowers the carbon dioxide level of the blood, which produces dizziness, tingling sensations, etc. *v.* **hy·per·ven·ti·lat·ed, hy·per·ven·ti·lat·ing. –hy′per·ven′ti·la′tion,** *n.*

hyp·o·crite (hip′ə krit), *n.* person who pretends to be what he or she is not, especially someone who claims to be very good or religious but does not act that way. [**Hypocrite** comes from a Greek word meaning "actor." Like actors, hypocrites pretend to be other than who they really are.]

hy·pot·e·nuse (hī pot′n üs), *n.* the side of a right triangle opposite the right angle.

hy·poth·e·sis (hī poth′ə sis), *n.* something assumed because it seems likely to be a true explanation; theory: *We began looking for her glasses with the hypothesis that they were probably in the living room somewhere.* ***n., pl.*** **hy·poth·e·ses** (hī poth′ə sēz′).

Ii

il·lu·sion·ist (i lü′zhə nist), *n.* person who produces misleading appearances or feelings; conjurer; magician.

im·mi·grate (im′ə grāt), *v.* to come into a country or region to live there. *v.* **im·mi·grat·ed, im·mi·grat·ing.**

im·mor·tal·ize (i môr′tl īz), *v.* **1.** to make immortal. **2.** to cause to be remembered or famous forever: *Great authors are immortalized by their works. v.* **im·mor·tal·ized, im·mor·tal·iz·ing. –im·mor′tal·i·za′tion,** *n.* **– im·mor′tal·iz′er,** *n.*

im·pact (im′pakt), **1.** *n.* action of striking one thing against another; collision: *The impact of the heavy stone against the windowpane shattered the glass.* **2.** *v.* to have an effect on: *choices that impact your life.* **–im·pac′tion,** *n.*

im·per·a·tive (im per′ə tiv), **1.** *adj.* not to be avoided; urgent; necessary: *It is imperative that this very sick child should stay in bed.* **2.** *n.* command: *The dog trainer issued sharp imperatives to the dog.* **–im·per′a·tive·ly,** *adv.* **–im·per′a·tive·ness,** *n.*

in·car·na·tion (in′kär nā′shən), *n.* **1.** someone who represents some quality or idea; embodiment: *The miser was an incarnation of greed.* **2.** act of taking on human form by a divine being: *the incarnation of an angel.*

in·def·i·nite (in def′ə nit), *adj.* **1.** not clearly defined; not exact: *indefinite instructions.* **2.** not limited: *We have an indefinite time to finish this work.* **–in·def′i·nite·ly,** *adv.* **–in·def′i·nite·ness,** *n.*

in·de·scrib·a·ble (in′di skrī′bə bəl), *adj.* not able to be described; beyond description: *a scene of indescribable beauty.* **–in′de·scrib′a·ble·ness,** *n.* **–in′de·scrib′a·bly,** *adv.*

in·dict·ment (in dīt′mənt), *n.* **1.** a formal written accusation, especially on the recommendation of a grand jury: *an indictment for murder.* **2.** accusation.

in·dig·e·nous (in dij′ə nəs), *adj.* originating or produced in a particular country; growing or living naturally in a certain region, soil, climate, etc.; native: *Lions are indigenous to Africa.* **–in·dig′e·nous·ly,** *adv.* [**Indigenous** comes from Latin words meaning "in" and "to give birth." Being indigenous to a place means having been born there.]

in·dig·nant·ly (in dig′nənt lē), *adv.* angrily; with anger at something unworthy, unjust, or mean.

in·ef·fec·tive (in′ə fek′tiv), *adj.* **1.** not producing the desired effect; of little use: *an ineffective medicine.* **2.** not able to do as well as expected; incapable: *Without the proper training, she was an ineffective supervisor.* **–in′ef·fec′tive·ly,** *adv.* **–in′ef·fec′tive·ness,** *n.*

in·e·qual·i·ty (in′i kwol′ə tē), *n.* **1.** lack of equality; condition of being unequal in amount, size, value, rank, etc: *There is a great inequality between the salaries of a bank president and a teller.* **2.** lack of evenness, regularity, or uniformity: *There are many inequalities in the New England coastline.* **3.** a mathematical expression showing that two quantities are unequal. EXAMPLES: *a>b means a is greater than b; a<b means a is less than b; a≠b means a and b are unequal.* *n., pl.* **in·e·qual·i·ties** *for 2, 3.*

in·er·tia (in ėr′shə), *n.* **1.** tendency of all objects and matter in the universe to stay still, or if moving, to go on moving in the same direction, unless acted on by some force. **2.** tendency to remain as before, and not start changes: *Only inertia, not shyness, keeps him from making new friends.*

in·fec·tion (in fek′shən), *n.* **1.** act or process of causing disease in people and other living things by bringing into contact with germs, viruses, fungi, etc. **2.** disease caused in this manner, especially one that can spread from one person to another.

in·fer·ence (in′fər əns), *n.* **1.** the process of inferring; finding out by reasoning: *What happened is only a matter of inference: no one saw the accident.* **2.** something that is inferred; conclusion: *What inference do you draw from smelling smoke?*

in·fin·ity (in fin′ə tē), *n.* **1.** condition of having no limits; endlessness: *The infinity of space.* **2.** an infinite extent, amount, number.

in·fir·mar·y (in fėr′mər ē), *n.* place for the care of the infirm, sick, or injured; hospital in a school or institution. *n., pl.* **in·fir·mar·ies.** [**Infirmary** comes from Latin words meaning "not" and "firm" or "healthy."]

in·frac·tion (in frak′shən), *n.* act of breaking a law or obligation; violation: *Reckless driving is an infraction of the law.*

in·no·va·tion (in′ə vā′shən), *n.* **1.** change made in the established way of doing things: *The principal made many innovations.* **2.** act or process of making changes; bringing in new things or new ways of doing things: *Many people are opposed to innovation.*

in·quir·y (in kwī′rē *or* in′kwər ē), *n.* **1.** question: *The guide answered all our inquiries.* **2.** a search for information, knowledge, or truth: *His inquiry into the town's history led him to many old books and newspapers.* *n., pl.* **in·quir·ies.**

in·scribe (in skrīb′), *v.* **1.** to write or engrave words, names, etc., on stone, metal, paper, etc.: *Her name was inscribed on the ring.* **2.** to mark stone, metal, paper, etc., with words, names, etc.: *The ring was inscribed with his name.* *v.* **in·scribed, in·scrib·ing. –in·scrib′er,** *n.*

in·spec·tor (in spek′tər), *n.* **1.** someone whose job is to carefully examine something: *The city building inspector told the landlord to fix the fire escape.* **2.** a police officer, usually ranking next below a superintendent.

in·te·ger (in′tə jər), *n.* any positive or negative whole number, or zero.

in·ten·si·ty (in ten′sə tē), *n.* **1.** quality of being intense; great strength: *The intensity of tropical sunlight.* **2.** extreme energy; great vigor; force: *intensity of thought, intensity of feeling.*

in·ter·cept (in′tər sept′), *v.* **1.** to take or seize on the way from one place to another: *intercept a letter, intercept a messenger, intercept a pass in a football game.* **2.** (in mathematics) to mark off part of a line or space between points or lines. A diameter of a circle intercepts the circumference at two points. [**Intercept** comes from Latin words meaning "to catch between."]

in·ter·est (in′tər ist), *n.* **1.** a feeling of wanting to know, see, do, own, share in, or take part in: *He has an interest in reading and in collecting stamps.* **2.** money paid for the use of someone else's money, usually a percentage of the amount invested, borrowed, or loaned: *The interest on the loan was 7 percent a year.* [**Interest** comes from a Latin word meaning "it matters." That Latin word comes from Latin words that mean "to be" and "between." Something between you and your goal probably matters to you.]

in·ter·jec·tion (in′tər jek′shən), *n.* **1.** an exclamation showing emotion. It is regarded as a part of speech. *Oh! ah! ouch!* and *hurrah!* are interjections. **2.** a sudden insertion into a conversation or speech: *The interjection of amusing stories into the speech made it more interesting.* **–in′ter·jec′tion·al,** *adj.*

in·ter·mi·na·ble (in tėr′mə nə bəl), *adj.* so long as to seem endless; very long and tiring. **–in·ter′mi·na·bly,** *adv.*

in·ter·mis·sion (in′tər mish′ən), *n.* **1.** interval between periods of activity; pause; interruption: *The band played from eight to twelve with a short intermission at ten.* **2.** stopping for a time; interruption: *The rain continued all day without intermission.*

in·ter·mit·tent (in′tər mit′nt), *adj.* stopping for a time and beginning again; not continuous: *The pilot watched for an intermittent red light, flashing on and off every 15 seconds.* **–in′ter·mit′tent·ly,** *adv.*

in·ter·rog·a·tive (in′tə rog′ə tiv), *adj.* **1.** asking a question; having the form of a question: *an interrogative sentence.* **2.** (in grammar) used in asking a question. *Where, when, why* are interrogative adverbs. *Who* and *what* are interrogative pronouns. **–in′ter·rog′a·tive·ly,** *adv.*

in·ter·stel·lar (in′tər stel′ər), *adj.* between the stars: *interstellar distances.*

in·ter·twine (in′tər twīn′), *v.* to twine, one with another: *Two vines intertwined on the wall.* *v.* **in·ter·twined, in·ter·twin·ing. –in′ter·twine′ment,** *n.*

in·ter·vene (in′tər vēn′), *v.* **1.** to come between persons or groups to help settle a dispute: *The President was asked to intervene in the coal strike.* **2.** to happen; take place so as to get in the way: *The parade was fun until bad weather intervened.* *v.* **in·ter·vened, in·ter·ven·ing. –in′ter·ve′nor** or **in′ter·ven′er,** *n.*

in·tra·mur·al (in′trə myůr′əl), *adj.* among students of the same school or college: *intramural sports.*

in·tra·net (in′trə net′), *n.* a computer network within one organization.

in·tra·per·son·al (in′trə pər′sən əl), *adj.* existing or occurring within one person's thoughts or self: *intrapersonal communication.*

in·tra·ve·nous (in′trə vē′nəs), *adj.* going into someone's body through a vein. *When a person is too ill to digest food, an intravenous feeding is often given.* **–in′tra·ve′nous·ly,** *adv.*

in·tro·duce (in′trə düs′), *v.* **1.** to bring into acquaintance with; make known: *I introduced my new friend to several of my old friends.* **2.** to bring into use, notice, knowledge, etc.: *introduce new products. Television and space travel are introducing many new words into our language.* *v.* **in·tro·duced, in·tro·duc·ing. –in′tro·duc′er,** *n.*

in·tro·duc·tor·y (in′trə duk′tə rē), *adj.* used to introduce; serving as an introduction; preliminary: *The speaker began her talk with a few introductory remarks about her subject.*

in·tro·spec·tive (in′trə spek′tiv), *adj.* inclined to examine your own thoughts and feelings. **–in′tro·spec′tive·ly,** *adv.*

in·tro·vert (in′trə vėrt′), *n.* person tending to think rather than act. Introverts are more interested in their own thoughts and feelings than in what is going on around them.

in·ven·tion (in ven′shən), *n.* **1.** something made for the first time: *Television is a twentieth-century invention.* **2.** act of making something new: *the invention of gunpowder.*

in·verse (in vėrs′ *or* in′vėrs′), **1.** *adj.* exactly opposite; reversed in position, direction, or tendency; inverted: *DCBA is the inverse order of ABCD.* **2.** *n.* something reversed: *Subtraction is the inverse of addition. The inverse of* $\frac{3}{4}$ *is* $\frac{4}{3}$. **–in·verse′ly,** *adv.*

in·vest·ment (in vest′mənt), *n.* **1.** act of investing; a laying out of money: *Getting an education is a wise investment of time and money.* **2.** something that is expected to yield money as income or profit or both: *She has a good income from wise investments.*

in·volve·ment (in volv′mənt), *n.* **1.** act or process of being drawn into a situation. **2.** the act of taking part in or participating in something.

i·so·la·tion·ism (i′sə lā′shə niz′əm), *n.* principles or policy of avoiding political alliances and economic relationships with other nations.

i·sos·ce·les (ī sos′ə lēz′), *n.* (isosceles triangle) a triangle that has two equal sides.

Jj

joule (jül *or* joul), *n.* unit of work equal to ten million ergs, or to the work done when a force of one newton moves an object one meter. Joules are used to measure all kinds of energy.

judg·ment (juj′mənt), *n.* **1.** result of judging; opinion or estimate: *In my judgment dogs make better pets than cats do.* **2.** ability to form sound opinions; power to judge well; good sense: *Since she has judgment in such matters, we will ask her.*

Kk

ki·net·ic (ki net′ik), *adj.* **1.** of motion. **2.** caused by motion.

kin·ship (kin′ship), *n.* **1.** family relationship. **2.** relationship. **3.** resemblance.

Ll

lab·o·ra·to·ry (lab′rə tôr′ē), *n.* **1.** place with apparatus for conducting scientific experiments, investigations, tests, etc.: *a chemical laboratory.* **2.** place for manufacturing drugs, medicines, chemicals, etc. *n., pl.* **lab·o·ra·to·ries.**

lig·a·ment (lig′ə mənt), *n.* band of strong tissue that connects bones or holds organs of the body in place. [**Ligament** comes from a Latin word meaning "to tie."]

lin·e·ar (lin′ē ər), *adj.* **1.** of a line or lines: *linear succession to the throne.* **2.** changing in a regular way or direction: *a story's linear development from beginning to end.* **–lin′e·ar·ly,** *adv.*

lit·i·ga·tion (lit′ə gā′shən), *n.* **1.** act of carrying on a lawsuit or going to law. **2.** a lawsuit or legal proceeding.

Mm

mag·net (mag′nit), *n.* **1.** piece of metal or ore that attracts iron of steel. A lodestone is a natural magnet. **2.** anything that attracts: *On hot days the swimming pool was a magnet for neighborhood children.*

mal·a·dy (mal′ə dē), *n.* **1.** any bodily disorder or disease: *Cancer and malaria are serious maladies.* **2.** any unwholesome or disordered condition: *Poverty and slums are social maladies. n., pl.* **mal·a·dies.**

ma·li·cious (mə lish′əs), *adj.* wishing to hurt or make suffer; spiteful: *That story is malicious gossip.* **–ma·li′cious·ly,** *adv.* **–ma·li′cious·ness,** *n.*

ma·lign (mə līn′), **1.** *v.* to speak evil of; slander: *You malign an honest person when you call that person a liar.* **2.** *adj.* evil; injurious: *Gambling can have a malign influence.* **–ma·lign′er,** *n.* **–ma·lign′ly,** *adv.*

mal·nour·ished (mal nėr′isht), *adj.* improperly fed or nurtured: *The stray cat looked malnourished.*

ma·neu·ver (mə nü′vər), **1.** *n.* a planned movement of troops or warships: *Every year the army and navy hold maneuvers for practice.* **2.** *v.* to move or handle skillfully: *I was able to maneuver the car through heavy traffic with ease.* **–ma·neu′ver·a·bil′i·ty,** *n.* **–ma·neu′ver·a·ble,** *adj.* **–ma·neu′ver·er,** *n.*

ma·nip·u·late (mə nip′yə lāt), *v.* **1.** to handle or treat, especially with skill: *She manipulated the controls of the airplane.* **2.** to manage by clever use of personal influence, especially unfair influence: *He manipulated the class so that he was elected president instead of his more qualified opponent. v.* **ma·nip·u·lat·ed, ma·nip·u·lat·ing.** **–ma·nip′u·la·tive,** *adj.* **–ma·nip′u·la·tor,** *n.*

man·u·al (man′yü əl), *adj.* **1.** of the hands: *Performing surgery requires manual skill.* **2.** done with the hands: *Digging a trench with a shovel is manual labor.* **–man′u·al·ly,** *adv.*

man·u·fac·ture (man′yə fak′chər), **1.** *v.* to make by hand or by machine. A big factory manufactures goods in large quantities by using machines and dividing the work among many people. **2.** *n.* act or process of making articles by hand or by machine, especially in large quantities. *v.* **man·u·fac·tured, man·u·fac·tur·ing.**

man·u·script (man′yə skript), *n.* a handwritten or keyboarded book or article. Manuscripts are sent to publishers to be made into printed books, magazine articles, and the like.

marriage (mar′ij), *n.* **1.** condition of living together as husband and wife; married life: *We wished the bride and groom a happy marriage.* **2.** the ceremony of being joined as husband and wife; act of marrying; wedding.

mass (mas), *n.* **1.** a lump: *a mass of dough.* **2.** the quantity of matter an object contains; the quality of a physical object that gives it inertia.The mass of an object is always the same on Earth, in outer space, etc.; its weight, which depends on the force of gravity, can vary. When the force of gravity does not vary, mass can be considered as weight, so units of mass are also used as units of weight. *n., pl.* **mass·es.**

me·chan·ics (mə kan′iks), *n.* **1.** *sing.* branch of physics dealing with the effects of forces applied to solid objects, liquid substances, or gases that are in motion or at rest. Mechanics was developed by Galileo, Newton, and others. **2.** *sing.* knowledge about machinery.

med·al·ist (med′l ist), *n.* someone who has won a medal: *an Olympic gold medalist in gymnastics.*

me·di·an (mē′dē ən), *n.* **1.** the middle number of a series: *The median of 1, 3, 4, 8, 9 is 4. The median of 8, 12, 16, 20 is 14.* **2.** a line from any angle of a triangle to the midpoint of the opposite side. **–me′di·an·ly,** *adv.*

mer·chants (mėr′chənts) *n.* **1.** people who buy and sell for profit; traders: *Some merchants do most of their business with foreign countries.* **2.** storekeepers.

met·a·phor (met′ə fôr), *n.* a figure of speech in which something is described by comparing it to something else, without using the words *like* or *as.* "A heart of stone" is a metaphor.

me·te·or (mē′tē ər), *n.* mass of stone or metal that enters Earth's atmosphere from outer space with enormous speed; shooting star. Meteors become so hot from rushing through the air that they glow and often burn up. [**Meteor** comes from a Greek word meaning "a thing in the air."]

me·te·or·ite (mē′tē ə rīt′), *n.* mass of stone or metal that has fallen from outer space to a planet or moon; a fallen meteor. [**Meteor** comes from a Greek word meaning "a thing in the air." **Meteorite** adds an ending meaning "rock."]

meter (mē′tər), *n.* the basic unit of length in the metric system.

mi·cro·cosm (mī′krō koz′əm), *n.* **1.** a little world; universe in miniature. **2.** someone or something thought of as a miniature representation of the universe.

mi·cro·phone (mī′krə fōn), *n.* device for magnifying or transmitting sounds by changing sound waves into electrical signals. Microphones are used for broadcasting and recording.

mi·gra·tion (mī grā′shən), *n.* **1.** act of going from one place or region to another: *Some kinds of birds travel thousands of miles on their migrations.* **2.** number of people or animals migrating together.

min·u·end (min′yü end), *n.* number or quantity from which another is to be subtracted: *In 100 – 23 = 77, the minuend is 100.*

mis·chie·vous (mis′chə vəs), *adj.* **1.** causing mischief; naughty: *mischievous behavior.* **2.** full of pranks and teasing fun: *mischievous children.* **–mis′chie·vous·ly,** *adv.* **–mis′chie·vous·ness,** *n.*

mis·cue (mis kyü′), *n.* error; mistake.

mis·giv·ing (mis giv′ing), *n.* a feeling of doubt, suspicion, or anxiety: *We started off through the storm with some misgivings.*

mis·judge (mis juj′), *v.* to judge wrongly or unjustly: *misjudge distance, misjudge a person's character. v.* **mis·judged, mis·judg·ing. –mis·judg′ment,** *n.*

mis·no·mer (mis nō′mər), *n.* **1.** name that describes wrongly: *"Lightning" is a misnomer for that old, slow horse.* **2.** error in naming. [**Misnomer** comes from French words meaning "wrongly" and "to name."]

mis·sion (mish′ən), *n.* **1.** errand or task that people are sent somewhere to do: *a diplomatic mission.* **2.** center or headquarters for religious or social work: *The church set up a mission with a soup kitchen to help local homeless people.* [**Mission** comes from a Latin word meaning "to send."]

mois·ture (mois′chər), *n.* slight wetness; water or other liquid suspended in very small drops in the air or spread on a surface. Dew is moisture that collects at night on the grass.

mo·men·tum (mō men′təm), *n.* **1.** amount measuring the motion of an object, equal to the product of its mass and its velocity: *A falling object gains momentum as it falls.* **2.** tendency to keep moving, resulting from movement: *The runner's momentum carried him far beyond the finish line.*

mon·arch (mon′ərk), *n.* **1.** king, queen, emperor, etc.; ruler. **2.** someone or something like a monarch: *The tall, solitary pine was monarch of the forest.* [**Monarch** comes from a Greek word meaning "alone." In old times, a monarch ruled alone, and a country has only one monarch at a time.]

mo·nop·o·ly (mə nop′ə lē), *n.* **1.** the complete control of a product or service: *The electric company has a monopoly on providing electrical service in the area it serves.* **2.** person or company that has a monopoly on some commodity or service. *n., pl.* **mo·nop·o·lies** for 2.

mor·tal (môr′tl), **1.** *adj.* sure to die sometime. **2.** *n.* a being that is sure to die sometime. All living creatures are mortals.

mor·tal·i·ty (môr tal′ə tē), *n.* **1.** mortal nature; being sure to die sometime. **2.** loss of life on a large scale: *The mortality from car accidents is dreadful.*

mort·gage (môr′gij) *n.* **1.** a loan made to the buyer of a building, or of land, used to pay for the property. The lender holds a claim to the property until the loan is repaid. **2.** document that gives such a claim. [**Mortgage** comes from French words meaning "dead" and "promise." When borrowed money is paid back as promised by a mortgage, the lender's claim on property ceases to exist, as if the claim were dead.]

mor·ti·cian (môr tish′ən), *n.* funeral director.

moun·tai·nous (moun′tə nəs), *adj.* **1.** covered with mountain ranges: *mountainous country.* **2.** huge: *a mountainous wave.* **–moun′tain·ous·ly,** *adv.*

mull (mul), *v.* to think about without making much progress; ponder.

mul·ti·me·di·a (mul′ti mē′dē ə), *adj.* using a combination of different media, such as tapes, films, compact disc recordings, and photographs, to entertain, communicate, teach, etc.: *Our presentation was a multimedia event.*

my·thol·o·gy (mi thol′ə jē), *n.* a group of myths about a particular country or person: *Greek mythology. n., pl.* **my·thol·o·gies.**

Nn

na·tion·al·ism (nash′ə nə liz′əm), *n.* **1.** patriotic feelings or efforts. **2.** desire and plans for national independence.

new·ton (nüt′n), *n.* unit for measuring force, used in the metric system. It is the amount of force required to give a mass of one kilogram an acceleration of one meter per second per second.

no·men·cla·ture (nō′men klā′chər), *n.* set or system of names or terms: *the nomenclature of music.*

nom·i·nal (nom′ə nəl), *adj.* **1.** existing in name only; not real: *The president is the nominal head of our club, but the secretary really runs things.* **2.** too small to be considered: *We paid our friend a nominal rent for the cottage—$25 a month.* **–nom′i·nal·ly,** *adv.*

nom·i·na·tive (nom′ə nə tiv), **1.** *adj.* showing the subject of a verb or the words agreeing with the subject. *I, he, she, we,* and *they* are in the nominative case. **2.** *n.* a word in the nominative case. *Who* and *I* are nominatives. **–nom′i·na·tive·ly,** *adv.*

non·cha·lant·ly (non′shə lənt lē), *adv.* calmly, without enthusiasm; coolly; indifferently. [**Nonchalant** comes from Latin words meaning "not" and "warm." Or as we say in English, cool.]

nu·ance (nü′äns *or* nü äns′), *n.* **1.** shade of expression, meaning, feeling, etc. **2.** shade of color or tone.

number line, *n.* line divided into equal segments by points corresponding to integers. The points to the right of 0 are positive; those to the left are negative. The set of all the points on the line corresponds to the set of real numbers.

nu·me·ra·tor (nü′mə rā′tər), *n.* number above or to the left of the line in a fraction, which shows how many equal parts of the whole make up the fraction: *In* $\frac{3}{8}$, *3 is the numerator and 8 is the denominator.*

nu·tri·ent (nü′trē ənt), *n.* any substance that a living thing needs to eat for energy, growth, and repair of tissues: *vitamins, minerals, and other nutrients.*

Oo

ob·li·ga·tion (ob′lə gā′shən), *n.* **1.** duty under the law or from personal feeling: *We have an obligation to help our friends when they need something.* **2.** act of binding yourself or condition of being bound by oath, promise, etc., to do something: *It was his obligation to return my favor.*

ob·sta·cle (ob′stə kəl), *n.* something that prevents or stops progress; hindrance: *A fallen tree was an obstacle to traffic. He overcame the obstacle of blindness and became a computer programmer.*

ob·struc·tion (əb struk′shən), *n.* **1.** something that is in the way; obstacle: *The old path was blocked by such obstructions as boulders and fallen trees.* **2.** act of process of blocking or hindering: *Obstruction of justice is a crime.*

ol·i·gar·chy (ol′ə gär′kē) *n.* **1.** form of government in which a few people have the ruling power. **2.** country or state having such a government. *n., pl.* **ol·i·gar·chies.** [**Oligarchy** comes from Greek words meaning "few" and "leader."]

op·por·tu·ni·ty (op′ər tü′nə tē), *n.* a good chance; favorable time; convenient occasion: *I had an opportunity to earn some money baby-sitting. n., pl.* **op·por·tu·ni·ties.**

op·po·site (op′ə zit) *adj.* **1.** placed directly across from something else; face to face; back to back: *The house straight across the street is opposite to ours.* **2.** as different as can be: *North and south are opposite directions. Sour is opposite to sweet.* **–op′po·site·ly,** *adv.* **–op′po·site·ness,** *n.*

op·pres·sion (ə presh′ən), *n.* **1.** cruel or unjust treatment; tyranny; persecution: *The oppression of the people by the invaders caused much suffering.* **2.** a heavy, weary feeling.

order of operations, *n.* rules that tell which calculation to perform first in a mathematical expression.

or·gan·ic (ôr gan′ik), *adj.* **1.** of or from living things: *organic fertilizer.* **2.** grown by using decaying things that were once alive instead of artificial fertilizers and pesticides: *organic foods.* **–or·gan′i·cal·ly,** *adv.*

o·zone (ō′zōn), *n.* a form of oxygen with a sharp, pungent odor, produced by electricity and especially present in the air after a thunderstorm. Ozone high in the atmosphere forms the protective ozone layer, but ozone near the ground pollutes the air, especially in smog.

Pp

par·al·lel·ism (par′ə lel′iz′əm), *n.* **1.** condition of being parallel. **2.** likeness; similarity; correspondence; agreement.

par·ti·ci·ple (pär′tə sip′əl), *n.* a verb form that keeps all the qualities of the verb, such as tense, voice, power to take an object, and modification by adverbs, but that may be used as an adjective. EXAMPLES: the students *writing* sentences at the blackboard, the people *waiting* for a train, the *polished* silver, the jewels *stolen* last night. In these phrases, *writing* and *waiting* are present participles; *polished* and *stolen* are past participles.

pas·sion·ate (pash′ə nit), *adj.* **1.** having or showing strong feelings: *She has always been a passionate believer in human rights.* **2.** resulting from strong feeling: *He made a passionate speech against death sentences.* **pas′sion·ate·ly,** *adv.* **–pas′sion·ate·ness,** *n.*

pa·thol·o·gy (pa thol′ə jē), *n.* **1.** study of the causes and nature of diseases. **2.** unhealthy conditions caused by a disease. *n., pl.* **pa·thol·o·gies** for 2. **–pa·thol′o·gist,** *n.*

pa·tri·ot·ism (pā′trē ə tiz′əm), *n.* love and loyal support of your country.

ped·es·tal (ped′i stəl), *n.* **1.** base on which a column or a statue stands. **2.** based of a tall vase, lamp, etc.

pe·des·tri·an (pə des′trē ən), **1.** *n.* person who goes on foot; walker: *Drivers should watch for pedestrians.* **2.** *adj.* going on foot; walking.

ped·i·cure (ped′ə kyůr), *n.* care or beauty treatment of the feet and toenails.

pe·dom·e·ter (pi dom′ə tər), *n.* device for recording the number of steps taken and thus measuring the distance traveled.

pel·vis (pel′vis), *n.* **1.** the basin-shaped cavity formed by the hipbones and the end of the backbone. **2.** bones forming this cavity. *n., pl.* **pel·vis·es, pel·ves** (pel′vēz).

per·il·ous (per′ə ləs), *adj.* full of peril; dangerous: *a perilous ocean voyage.* **–per′il·ous·ly,** *adv.* **–per′il·ous·ness,** *n.*

pe·rim·e·ter (pə rim′ə tər), *n.* **1.** the outer boundary of a figure or area: *the perimeter of a circle, the perimeter of a garden.* **2.** distance around such a boundary. The perimeter of a square equals four times the length of one side.

per·i·od·i·cal (pir′ē od′ə kəl), **1.** *n.* magazine that is published at regular times, less often than daily: *This periodical comes out monthly.* **2.** *adj.* published at regular intervals, less often than daily.

per·sist·ence (pər sis′təns), *n.* **1.** act of refusing to stop or be changed: *I was annoyed by the persistence of a fly buzzing around my head.* **2.** a continuing existence: *the persistence of a cough.*

per·son·i·fy (pər son′ə fī), *v.* **1.** to be a type of; embody: *Hitler and Stalin personified evil.* **2.** to regard or represent as a person. We personify time and nature when we refer to *Father Time* and *Mother Nature. v.* **per·son·i·fied, per·son·i·fy·ing. –per·son′i·fi′er,** *n.*

phon·ics (fon′iks), *n.* simplified phonetics, or the science dealing with sounds made in speech and the art of pronunciation, for teaching reading.

pil·grim (pil′grəm), *n.* **1.** person who goes on a journey to a sacred or holy place as an act of religious devotion. In the Middle Ages, many people went as pilgrims to Jerusalem and to holy places in Europe. **2.** traveler; wanderer.

pil·grim·age (pil′grə mij), *n.* **1.** a pilgrim's journey; a journey to some sacred place as an act of religious devotion. **2.** a long journey.

pla·gia·rism (plā′jə riz′əm), *n.* act of taking and using as your own the thoughts, writings, etc., of another, especially taking and using a passage, plot, etc., from the work of another writer.

plas·ma (plaz′mə), *n.* the clear, very pale, yellowish liquid part of blood or lymph. Blood cells float in this liquid.

plau·si·ble (plò′zə bəl), *adj.* **1.** appearing true, reasonable, or fair. **2.** apparently worthy of confidence but often not really so: *a plausible liar.* **–plau′si·bil′i·ty, plau′si·ble·ness,** *n.* **–plau′si·bly,** *adv.*

plead (plēd), *v.* **1.** to offer reasons for or against; argue. **2.** to ask earnestly; make an earnest appeal: *When the rent was due, the poor family pleaded for more time. v.* **plead·ed** or **pled, plead·ing. –plead′a·ble,** *adj.* **–plead′er,** *n.* **–plead′ing·ly,** *adv.*

plu·to·crat (plü′tə krat), *n.* **1.** person who has power or influence because of wealth. **2.** a wealthy person.

po·di·a·trist (pə dī′ə trist), *n.* person who is an expert in the branch of medicine that studies and treats diseases and problems of the human foot.

po·di·um (pō′dē əm), *n.* a raised platform. The conductor of an orchestra or a speaker before an audience often stands on a podium. *n., pl.* **po·di·ums, po·di·a** (pō′dē ə). [**Podium** comes from a Greek word meaning "foot." A podium is a place to stand.]

pol·lu·tion (pə lü′shən), *n.* **1.** act or process of dirtying any part of the environment, especially with waste material. **2.** anything that dirties the environment, especially waste material: *pollution of the air, pollution at the beach.* **–pol·lu·tion′-free′,** *adj.*

pol·y·gon (pol′ē gon), *n.* a closed plane figure with three or more straight sides and angles.

pol·y·he·dron (pol′ē hē′drən), *n.* a solid figure having four or more faces. *n., pl.* **pol·y·he·drons, pol·y·he·dra** (pol′ē hē′drə).

pon·der (pon′dər), *v.* to consider carefully; think over; *ponder a problem.* **–pon′der·er,** *n.*

pop·u·lar (pop′yə lər), *adj.* **1.** liked by most people: *a popular song.* **2.** liked by acquaintances or associates: *Her good nature makes her the most popular girl in the class.* **–pop′u·lar·ly,** *adv.*

pop·u·lar·i·ty (pop′yə lar′ə tē), *n.* fact or condition of being liked by most people.

pop·u·la·tion (pop′yə lā′shən), *n.* **1.** people of a city, country, or district. **2.** the number of people living in a place.

pop·u·lous (pop′yə ləs), *adj.* full of people; having many people per square mile. **–pop′u·lous·ly,** *adv.* **–pop′u·lous·ness,** *n.*

por·ter (pôr′tər), *n.* **1.** person employed to carry loads or baggage: *Give your bags to the porter.* **2.** attendant in a parlor car or sleeping car of a passenger train.

port·fo·li·o (pôrt fō′lē ō), *n.* **1.** a portable case for loose papers, drawings, etc. **2.** a set of drawings, photographs, etc., that show an artist's or model's work, usually carried in a large folder. *n., pl.* **port·fo·li·os.**

pos·ses·sive (pə zes′iv) *adj.* **1.** showing possession. *My, your, his,* and *our* are in the possessive case because they indicate who possesses or owns. **2.** desirous of ownership: *She is very possessive of her books and will not lend them.* **–pos·ses′sive·ly,** *adv.* **–pos·ses′sive·ness,** *n.*

post·date (pōst′dāt′), *v.* **1.** to give a later date than the true date to a letter, check, etc. **2.** to follow in time. *v.* **post·dat·ed, post·dat·ing.**

post·pone (pōst pōn′), *v.* to put something off till later; put off to a later time; delay: *The softball game was postponed because of rain.* *v.* **post·poned, post·pon·ing. –post·pone′ment,** *n.* **–post·pon′er,** *n.*

post·sea·son (pōst′sē′zən), *n.* time after the regular period for games and competitions in a sport, in which playoffs or additional games are held.

post·war (pōst′wôr′), *adj.* after the war.

prec·e·dent (pres′ə dənt *for noun;* pri sēd′nt *or* pres′ə dənt *for adj.*), **1.** *n.* action that may serve as an example or reason for a later action: *A decision of a court often serves as a precedent in other courts. Last year's school picnic set a precedent for having one this year.* **2.** *adj.* preceding.

pre·cip·i·ta·tion (pri sip′ə tā′shən), *n.* **1.** the act or process of falling from the air in the form of rain, snow, etc. **2.** the amount of water that falls from the air in a certain time.

pred·e·ces·sor (pred′ə ses′ər), *n.* any person or thing that came before another, performing the same functions, or having the same title or office.

pre·de·ter·mine (prē′di tėr′mən), *v.* to determine or decide beforehand: *We met at the predetermined time.* *v.* **pre·de·ter·mined, pre·de·ter·min·ing. –pre′de·ter′mi·na′tion,** *n.*

pref·ace (pref′is), **1.** *n.* introduction to a book, writing, or speech: *My history book has a preface written by the author.* **2.** *v.* to introduce by written or spoken remarks; give a preface to: *He prefaced his speech with a joke about the weather.* *v.* **pref·aced, pref·ac·ing.**

pre·fix (prē′fiks), *n.* syllable, syllables, or word put at the beginning of a word to change its meaning or to make another word, as *pre-* in *prepaid, under-* in *underline, dis-* in *disappear, un-* in *unlike,* and *re-* in *redo. n., pl.* **pre·fix·es.**

pre·his·to·ric (prē′hi stôr′ik), *adj.* of or belonging to times before histories were written: *Prehistoric peoples used stone tools.* **–pre′his·to′ri·cal·ly,** *adv.*

prej·u·dice (prej′ə dis) *n.* **1.** unreasonable dislike of an idea, group of people, etc. **2.** opinion formed without sufficient knowledge or taking time and care to judge the facts fairly: *a prejudice against unfamiliar foods.* *v.* **prej·u·diced, prej·u·dic·ing.**

pre·mo·ni·tion (prē′mə nish′ən *or* prem′ə nish′ən), *n.* a forewarning: *a vague premonition of disaster.*

prep·o·si·tion (prep′ə zish′ən), *n.* word that expresses some relation to a noun, pronoun, phrase, or clause which follows it. *With, for, by,* and *in* are prepositions in the sentence "A man *with* vegetables *for* sale drove *by* our house *in* the morning."

pre·scribe (pri skrīb′), *v.* **1.** to order as a medicine or treatment: *The doctor prescribed penicillin.* **2.** to lay down as a rule to be followed; order; direct: *Good citizens do what the laws prescribe.* *v.* **pre·scribed, pre·scrib·ing. –pre·scrib′er,** *n.*

pre·vent·a·ble (pri vent′ə bəl), *adj.* capable of being kept from happening.

pro·ac·tive (prō ak′tiv), *adj.* acting in anticipation of a future situation; acting to control a problem before it occurs.

pro·ce·dure (prə sē′jər), *n.* **1.** way of proceeding; method of doing things: *What is your procedure in making bread?* **2.** the customary manners or ways of conducting business: *parliamentary procedure, legal procedure.* **–pro·ce′dur·al,** *adj.*

pro·ceed·ings (prə sē′dingz), *n.* **1.** action in a case in a court of law. **2.** record of what was done at the meetings of a society, club, etc.

pro·cras·ti·nate (prō kras′tə nāt), *v.* to put things off until later; delay. *v.* **pro·cras·ti·nat·ed, pro·cras·ti·nat·ing. –pro·cras′ti·na′tion,** *n.* **–pro·cras′ti·na′tor,** *n.*

pro·duc·tiv·i·ty (prō′duk tiv′ə tē), *n.* power to produce; productiveness.

pro·fi·cient (prə fish′ənt), *adj.* very skilled or knowledgeable in any art, science, or subject; expert: *to be proficient in mathematics.* **–pro·fi′cient·ly,** *adv.* **–pro·fi′cient·ness,** *n.*

pro·gram·mer (prō′gram′ər), *n.* person who prepares a computer program or programs.

pro·gres·sive (prə gres′iv), *adj.* **1.** making progress; advancing toward something better; improving: *a progressive nation.* **2.** favoring progress; wanting improvement or reform in government, business, etc. **–pro·gres′sive·ly,** *adv.* **–pro·gres′sive·ness,** *n.*

proj·ect (proj′ekt *for noun;* prə jekt′ *for verb*), **1.** *n.* a plan; scheme; effort; undertaking: *a project for better sewage disposal.* **2.** *v.* to throw or cast forward: *A cannon projects shells.*

pro·jec·tion (prə jek′shən), *n.* **1.** part that projects or sticks out: *rocky projections on the face of a cliff.* **2.** act of throwing or casting forward: *the projection of a photographic image on a screen.*

prom·e·nade (prom′ə nād′ *or* prom′ə näd′) *n.* **1.** a walk for pleasure or for show: *They took a promenade in their fine clothes.* **2.** a public place for such a walk: *Atlantic City has a famous promenade along the beach.* **–prom′e·nad′er,** *n.*

prop·er·ty (prop′ər tē), *n.* **1.** thing or things owned: possession or possessions: *This house is that man's property. That book is my property; please return it to me.* **2.** quality or power belonging specially to something: *Copper has several important properties. n., pl.* **prop·er·ties** for 2.

pro·po·nent (prə pō′nənt), *n.* person who supports something; advocate: *Both candidates are proponents of more funds for schools.*

pro·por·tion·al (prə pôr′shə nəl), *adj.* **1.** in the proper proportion; corresponding: *The pay will be proportional to the amount of time put in.* **2.** (in mathematics) having the same relationship in size. **–pro·por′tion·al·ly,** *adv.*

prop·o·si·tion (prop′ə zish′ən), *n.* **1.** what is offered to be considered; proposal: *The corporation presented a proposition to buy several smaller businesses.* **2.** statement. EXAMPLE: "All men are created equal."

prose (prōz), **1.** *n.* the ordinary form of spoken or written language; plain language not arranged in verses. **2.** *adj.* of or in prose. [**Prose** comes from a Latin word meaning "straight." Latin poetry and English poetry often use words in fancy or complicated ways. Prose is more direct, like a straight road compared to a winding one.]

pros·pect (pros′pekt) *n.* **1.** thing expected or looked forward to: *The prospects from our gardens are good this year.* **2.** act of looking forward; expectation: *The prospect of a vacation is pleasant.*

pro·tag·o·nist (prō tag′ə nist), *n.* the main character in a play, story, or novel.

psy·chol·o·gist (sī kol′ə jist), *n.* expert in psychology, the science of the mind.

pub·li·ca·tion (pub′lə kā′shən), *n.* **1.** book, newspaper, or magazine; anything that is published. **2.** the printing and selling of books, newspapers, magazines, etc.

pub·li·cize (pub′lə sīz), *v.* to give publicity, or public notice gained by giving out information, to. *v.* **pub·li·cized, pub·li·ciz·ing.**

pub·lish (pub′lish), *v.* **1.** to prepare and offer a book, newspaper, magazine, sheet music, or other printed material for sale or distribution. **2.** to make publicly or generally known: *Don't publish the faults of your friends.* **–pub′lish·a·ble,** *adj.*

pyr·a·mid (pir′ə mid) *n.* **1.** a solid figure having a polygon for a base and triangular sides which meet in a point. **2.** anything having the form of a pyramid: *a pyramid of stones.*

Qq

quad·rant (kwäd′rənt), *n.* **1.** quarter of the circumference of a circle; arc of 90 degrees. **2.** one of the four parts into which a plane is divided by two perpendicular lines.

quan·ti·ta·tive (kwän′tə tā′tiv), *adj.* **1.** concerned with quantity or quantities, or numbers and amounts. **2.** measurable. **–quan′ti·ta′tive·ly,** *adv.*

quar·tile (kwôr tīəl), *n.,* each of the three values that divide the items of frequency distribution into four classes with each containing one fourth of the total population.

quer·y (kwir′ē), **1.** *n.* a question; inquiry. **2.** *v.* to ask; ask about; inquire into: *The teacher queried my reason for being late. n., pl.* **quer·ies,** *v.* **quer·ied, quer·y·ing. –quer′i·er,** *n.*

quest (kwest), **1.** *n.* a search or hunt: *She went to the library on a quest for something to read.* **2.** *v.* to search or seek for; hunt. **–quest′er,** *n.*

ques·tion·a·ble (kwes′chə nə bəl), *adj.* **1.** open to question or dispute; doubtful; uncertain: *a questionable statement.* **2.** of doubtful honesty, morality, etc.: *questionable behavior.* **–ques′tion·a·ble·ness,** *n.* **–ques′tion·a·bly,** *adv.*

quo·tient (kwō′shənt), *n.* number arrived at by dividing one number by another. In $26 \div 2 = 13$, 13 is the quotient.

Rr

rational number, *n.* any number that can be expressed as an integer or as a ratio between two integers, excluding zero as a denominator. The numbers 2, 5, and $\frac{1}{2}$ are rational numbers.

ray (rā), *n.* **1.** a beam of light: *rays of the sun.* **2.** the part of a line on one side of any particular point on the line; half-line. [**Ray** comes from a Latin word meaning "spoke of a wheel."]

re·al·ist (rē′ə list), *n.* **1.** person interested in what is real and practical rather than what is imaginary or theoretical. **2.** artist or writer who represents things as they are in real life.

re·claim (ri klām′), *v.* **1.** to bring back to or put into a useful, good condition: *The farmer reclaimed the eroded land by terracing it and applying topsoil.* **2.** to demand or ask for the return of: *We reclaimed our luggage at the end of the trip.* **–re·claim′a·ble,** *adj.* **–re·claim′er,** *n.*

rec·la·ma·tion (rek′lə mā′shən), *n.* restoration to a useful, good condition: *the reclamation of deserts by irrigation.*

rec·tan·gle (rek′tang′gəl), *n.* a four-sided plane figure with four right angles. [**Rectangle** comes from a Latin word meaning "to keep straight."]

rec·ti·fy (rek′tə fī), *v.* **1.** to make right; put right; adjust; remedy: *The storekeeper admitted his mistake and was willing to rectify it.* **2.** to purify or refine: *rectify a liquor by distilling it several times. v.* **rec·ti·fied, rec·ti·fy·ing. –rec′ti·fi′a·ble,** *adj.* **–rec′ti·fi·ca′tion,** *n.*

ref·er·ence (ref′ər əns), **1.** *n.* act of calling someone's attention to something: *references to newspaper articles.* **2.** *adj.* used for information or help: *The reference librarian can find the article you're looking for.*

re·frac·tion (ri frak′shən), *n.* act or process of bending a ray of light, sound waves, etc., when passing from one medium into another of different density.

ref·u·gee (ref′yə jē′ *or* ref′yə jē′), *n.* a person who flees for refuge or safety, especially to a foreign country, in time of persecution, war, or disaster. *Refugees from the war were cared for in neighboring countries. n., pl.* **ref·u·gees.**

re·gress (ri gres′), *v.* to return to an earlier condition or stage of development. **–re·gres′sion,** *n.* **–re·gres′sor,** *n.*

re·new (ri nü′), *v.* **1.** to make new again; make like new; restore: *Rain renews the garden.* **2.** to begin again; get again; say, do, or give again: *He renewed his efforts to open the window.* **–re·new′er,** *n.*

re·plen·ish (ri plen′ish), *v.* to fill again; provide a new supply for: *Once our natural resources are used up we cannot replenish them.* **–re·plen′ish·er,** *n.* **–re·plen′ish·ment,** *n.*

re·pres·sion (ri presh′ən), *n.* **1.** act of preventing from acting or putting down: *The repression of a laugh made him choke.* **2.** condition of preventing from acting or putting down: *Repression made the people revolt against the government.*

re·pro·duce (rē′prə düs′), *v.* **1.** to make a copy of: *to reproduce a photograph.* **2.** to produce again; make or create over: *to reproduce music from a recording. v.* **re·pro·duced, re·pro·duc·ing, –re′pro·duc′er,** *n.* **–re′pro·duc′i·ble,** *adj.*

re·pub·lic (ri pub′lik), *n.* **1.** government in which the citizens elect representatives to manage the government, which is usually headed by a president. **2.** nation or state that has such a government. The United States and Mexico are republics.

req·ui·si·tion (rek′wə zish′ən), **1.** *v.* to demand or take by authority: *requisition supplies.* **2.** *n.* a demand made, especially a formal, written demand: *The principal signed a requisition for new books.*

res·i·due (rez′ə dü), *n.* what remains after a part is taken; remainder. *His will directed that after the payment of all debts the residue of his property should go to his children. The syrup dried up, leaving a sticky residue.*

res·o·lu·tion (rez′ə lü′shən), *n.* **1.** decision; making up your mind to do or not do something: *We made a resolution to get up early.* **2.** answer or solution: *the resolution of a problem, the resolution of a plot in a novel.*

ret·i·na (ret′n ə), *n.* inner membrane at the back of the eyeball that is sensitive to light and receives the images of things looked at. The retina transmits these images to the brain through the optic nerve. *n., pl.* **ret·i·nas.**

re·trac·tion (ri trak′shən), *n.* **1.** act of taking back; withdrawal of a promise, statement, etc.: *The newspaper published a retraction of the inaccurate report about the actress.* **2.** act of drawing or condition of being drawn back or in.

ret·ro·ac·tive (ret′rō ak′tiv), *adj.* having an effect on what is past. A retroactive law applies to events that occurred before the law was passed. **–ret′ro·ac′tive·ly,** *adv.* **–ret′ro·ac·tiv′i·ty,** *n.*

ret·ro·grade (ret′rə grād), **1.** *adj.* moving backward; retreating. **2.** *v.* to fall back toward a worse condition; grow worse; decline. *v.* **ret·ro·grad·ed, ret·ro·grad·ing. –ret′ro·grade′ly,** *adv.*

ret·ro·spect (ret′rə spekt), *n.* survey of past time, events, etc.; thinking about the past.

rev·e·nue (rev′ə nü), *n.* money coming in; income: *The government gets revenue from taxes.*

re·vers·i·ble (ri vėr′sə bəl), *adj.* **1.** able to be turned backward, or in the opposite position or direction. **2.** (of a garment, fabric, etc.) finished on both sides so that it can be worn with either side showing.

re·vert (ri vėrt′), *v.* to go back; return: *My thoughts reverted to the last time that I had seen her.*

re·volve (ri volv′), *v.* **1.** to move in a circle; move in a curve round a point: *The moon revolves around Earth.* **2.** to turn round a center or axis; rotate: *The wheels of a moving car revolve. v.* **re·volved, re·volv·ing. –re·volv′a·ble,** *adj.* [**Revolve** comes from a Latin word meaning "to roll."]

rhet·or·ic (ret′ər ik), *n.* **1.** art of using words effectively in speaking or writing. **2.** speech that sounds important, but is actually meaningless or insincere.

rhom·bus (rom′bəs), *n.* parallelogram with equal sides, usually having two obtuse angles and two acute angles. *n., pl.* **rhom·bus·es, rhom·bi** (rhom′bī).

ru·bric (rü′brik), *n.* **1.** title or heading of a chapter, a law, etc., written or printed in red or in special lettering. **2.** rule for the conducting of religious services inserted in a prayer book, ritual, etc. **3.** any heading, rule, or guide. [**Rubric** comes from a Latin word that means "red coloring matter."]

rum·mage (rum′ij), *v.* **1.** to search thoroughly by moving things about: *I rummaged through three drawers before I found my gloves.* **2.** to search in a disorderly way: *He rummaged in the drawer for a sheet of paper.* *v.* **rum·maged, rum·mag·ing. –rum′mag·er,** *n.*

Ss

sal·u·ta·tion (sal′yə tā′shən), *n.* **1.** act of greeting or saluting: *The man raised his hand in salutation.* **2.** something said, written, or done as a sign of welcome, farewell, or honor: *Begin your letter with the salutation "Dear Sir." A curtsy was her parting salutation.*

sam·ple (sam′pəl), **1.** *n.* part to show what the rest is like; one thing to show what the others are like: *Here are some samples of drapery material for you to choose from.* **2.** *v.* to take a part of; test a part of: *We sampled the cake and found it very good.* *v.* **sam·pled, sam·pling.**

sanc·tu·ar·y (sangk′chü er′ē), *n.* **1.** a sacred place. A church is a sanctuary. **2.** place of refuge or protection: *a wildlife sanctuary.* *n., pl.* **sanc·tu·ar·ies.**

saun·ter (sȯn′tər), **1.** *v.* to walk along slowly and happily; stroll: *People sauntered through the park on summer evenings.* **2.** *n.* a stroll. **–saun′ter·er.**

scale drawing, *n.* a picture or diagram of a place or object with dimensions reduced in size but proportional to the place or object's actual dimensions.

sca·lene (skā lēn′ *or* skā′lēn′), *adj.* (of a triangle) having three sides unequal.

scrip·ture (skrip′chər), *n.* any sacred writing.

scur·ry (skėr′ē), **1.** *v.* to run quickly; scamper; hurry: *Mice scurry in the walls.* **2.** *n.* act of scurrying: *With much fuss and scurry, they at last got started.* *v.* **scur·ried, scur·ry·ing.**

se·cede (si sēd′), *v.* to withdraw formally from an organization. *v.* **se·ced·ed, se·ced·ing. –se·ced′er,** *n.*

sen·si·tive (sen′sə tiv), *adj.* **1.** receiving impressions readily: *The eye is sensitive to light.* **2.** aware of the feelings and needs of other people. **–sen′si·tive·ly,** *adv.* **–sen′si·tive·ness,** *n.*

se·quen·tial (si kwen′shəl), *adj.* forming a sequence or connected series. **–se·quen′tial·ly,** *adv.*

sim·i·le (sim′ə lē′), *n.* a statement that one thing is like another. EXAMPLES: a face like marble, as brave as a lion.

simple interest, *n.* interest paid only on the original sum of money borrowed or invested, not on the interest that has grown since.

smirk (smėrk), **1.** *v.* to smile in a silly or self-satisfied way. **2.** *n.* a silly or self-satisfied smile.

smug·ly (smug′ lē), *adv.* in a manner expressing too much pleasure in your own goodness, cleverness, respectability, etc.; in a self-satisfied manner; complacently.

so·cia·ble (sō′shə bəl), *adj.* **1.** liking company; friendly: *They are a sociable family and entertain a great deal.* **2.** marked by conversation and companionship: *We had a sociable afternoon together.* **–so′cia·bil′i·ty,** *n.* **–so′cia·bly,** *adv.*

so·cial·ist (sō′shə list), **1.** *n.* person who favors or supports the theory or system of social organization by which the major means of production and distribution are owned, managed, or controlled by the government, by associations of workers, or by the community as a whole. **2.** *adj.* socialistic.

so·cial·ized (sō′shə līzd), *v.* **1.** was social or friendly: *He never socialized with his fellow workers.* **2.** made to be friendly or enjoy the company of others; made fit for living with others. *v.* **so·cial·iz·ing. –so′cial·i·za′tion,** *n.* **–so′cial·iz′er,** *n.*

so·ci·e·ty (sə sī′ə tē), *n.* **1.** all the people; human beings living together as a group: *Society must work hard for world peace.* **2.** group of persons joined together for a common purpose by a common interest. *n., pl.* **so·ci·e·ties** for 2.

so·ci·ol·o·gy (sō′sē ol′ə jē), *n.* study of the nature, origin, and development of human society and community life; science of society. Sociology deals with social conditions, such as crime and poverty, and social institutions, such as marriage, the family, and the school. **–so′ci·ol′o·gist,** *n.*

so·ci·o·path (sō′sē ə path), *n.* person who lacks any sense of social or moral responsibility toward others; antisocial person.

sol·ace (sol′is), **1.** *n.* comfort or relief: *She found solace from her troubles in music.* **2.** *v.* to comfort or relieve; cheer: *He solaced himself with a book.* *v.* **sol·aced, sol·ac·ing. –sol′ac·er,** *n.*

spec·i·men (spes′ə mən), *n.* **1.** one of a group or class taken to show what the others are like; sample: *He collects specimens of all kinds of rocks and minerals. The statue was a fine specimen of Greek sculpture.* **2.** samples of blood, urine, etc., for analysis or examination.

spectacular|tendon

spec·tac·u·lar (spek tak′yə lər), *adj.* **1.** making a great display: *the spectacular eruption of a volcano.* **2.** of or about a public display or show. **–spec·tac′u·lar·ly,** *adv.*

spec·u·late (spek′yə lāt), *v.* **1.** to think carefully; reflect; meditate; consider: *The philosopher speculated about time and space.* **2.** to guess; conjecture: *She tried to speculate about the possible winner.* *v.* **spec·u·lat·ed, spec·u·lat·ing.**

sput·ter (sput′ər), *v.* **1.** to make spitting or popping noises: *fat sputtering in the frying pan. The firecrackers sputtered.* **2.** to talk in a hasty confused way: *Embarrassed, he began to sputter and make silly excuses.* **–sput′ter·er,** *n.*

stan·za (stan′zə), *n.* group of lines of poetry, usually four or more, arranged according to a fixed plan; verse of a poem: *They sang the first and last stanzas of "America."* *n., pl.* **stan·zas.**

stel·lar (stel′ər), *adj.* **1.** of or like the stars or a star. **2.** leading; main; chief; *a stellar role.*

ster·num (stėr′nəm), *n.* breastbone. *n., pl.* **sternums** or **ster·na** (stėr′nə).

stock·hold·er (stok′hōl′dər), *n.* owner of stocks or shares in a company.

strat·o·sphere (strat′ə sfir *or* strā′tə sfir), *n.* region of the atmosphere between the troposphere and the mesosphere, extending from about 10 to 35 miles (16 to 56 kilometers) above Earth's surface. In the stratosphere, temperature varies little with changes in altitude, and the winds are mostly horizontal. **–strat′o·spher′ic,** *adj.*

sub·con·tract (sub kon′trakt), **1.** *n.* contract for carrying out a previous contract or part of it: *The contractor for the new building gave out subcontracts to a plumber and an electrician.* **2.** *v.* to make a subcontract.

sub·or·di·nate (sə bôrd′n it), *adj.* **1.** lower in rank: *In the military, lieutenants are subordinate to captains.* **2.** having less importance; secondary; dependent: *An assistant has a subordinate position.*

sub·scribe (səb skrīb′), *v.* **1.** to promise to take and pay for: *We subscribe to a few magazines.* **2.** to promise to give or pay a sum of money: *She subscribed $50 to the hospital fund.* *v.* **sub·scribed, sub·scrib·ing. –sub·scrib′er,** *n.*

sub·scrip·tion (səb skrip′shən), *n.* **1.** the right to receive something, obtained by paying a certain sum: *Our subscription to the newspaper expires next week.* **2.** act of subscribing.

sub·stance (sub′stəns), *n.* material that something is made of; matter: *Ice and water are the same substance in different forms.*

sub·ter·ra·ne·an (sub′tə rā′nē ən), *adj.* **1.** underground: *A subterranean passage led from the castle to a cave.* **2.** carried on secretly; hidden: *subterranean plotting.*

suc·ces·sion (sək sesh′ən), *n.* **1.** group of things happening one after another; series: *A succession of accidents spoiled our trip.* **2.** act or process in which one person or thing comes after another.

sus·pi·cion (sə spish′ən), *n.* **1.** belief; feeling; thought: *I have a suspicion that the weather will be very hot today.* **2.** state of mind of someone who suspects; act of suspecting: *The real thief tried to turn suspicion toward others.*

sus·pi·cious (sə spish′əs), *adj.* **1.** feeling suspicion; suspecting: *Our dog is suspicious of strangers.* **2.** causing someone to suspect: *a suspicious manner.* **–sus·pi′cious·ly,** *adv.* **–sus·pi′cious·ness,** *n.*

syl·lab·i·ca·tion (sə lab′ə kā′shən), *n.* the act or process of dividing into syllables, or parts of a word.

sym·bol·ism (sim′bə liz′əm), *n.* **1.** use of symbols, or things that stand for something else; representation by symbols. **2.** system of symbols: *The cross, the crown, the lamb, and the lily are parts of Christian symbolism.*

sys·tem·at·ic (sis′tə mat′ik), *adj.* **1.** according to a system; having a system, method, or plan: *systematic work.* **2.** orderly in arranging things or in getting things done: *a systematic person.* **–sys′tem·at′i·cal·ly,** *adv.*

Tt

tech·no·crat (tek′nə krat), *n.* person in favor of a government by mechanical or industrial experts.

tech·nol·o·gy (tek nol′ə jē), *n.* **1.** the use of scientific knowledge to control physical objects and forces: *overcome problems by technology.* **2.** any method for carrying out a process involving physical objects and forces: *the technology of weaving.* **–tech·nol′o·gist,** *n.*

tech·no·pho·bi·a (tek′nə fō′bē ə), *n.* fear of using technology or of the effects of technology. **–tech′no·pho·bic,** *adj.*

tel·e·gram (tel′ə gram), *n.* coded message sent over wires by means of electrical signals: *receive a telegram.*

tel·e·graph (tel′ə graf), *n.* **1.** way of sending coded messages over wires by means of electrical signals. **2.** device used for sending these messages. **–te·leg·ra·pher** (tə leg′rə fər), *n.*

tend·en·cy (ten′dən sē), *n.* a natural inclination to do something: *a tendency to oversleep. Wood has a tendency to swell if it gets wet.* *n., pl.* **tend·en·cies.**

ten·don (ten′dən), *n.* a tough, strong band or cord of tissue that joins a muscle to a bone or some other body part.

ten·dril (ten′drəl), *n.* **1.** a threadlike part of a climbing plant that attaches itself to something and helps support the plant. **2.** something like this part of a plant: *curly tendrils of hair.*

ten·sion (ten′shən), *n.* **1.** mental strain: *Tension is sometimes brought on by overwork.* **2.** situation in which people or groups are nervous or hostile toward each other: *political tension.* **–ten′sion·al,** *adj.* **–ten′sion·less,** *adj.*

term (tėrm), *n.* **1.** word or phrase used in connection with some special subject, science, art, or business: *medical terms.* "Acid," "base," and "salt" are terms commonly used in chemistry. **2.** a set period of time; length of time that a thing lasts: *The President's term of office is four years.* [**Term** comes from a Latin word meaning "end" or "boundary line."]

ter·mi·nate (tėr′mə nāt), *v.* **1.** to bring to an end; put an end to: *The two lawyers terminated their partnership and each opened a separate office.* **2.** to come to an end: *The contract terminates soon.* *v.* **ter·mi·nat·ed, ter·mi·nat·ing. –ter′mi·na′tion,** *n.* **–ter′mi·na′tor,** *n.* [**Terminator** comes from a Latin word meaning "end" or "boundary line."]

ter·race (ter′is), *n.* **1.** a flat, raised level of land with straight or sloping sides. Terraces are often made one above the other in hilly areas to create more space for raising crops. **2.** a paved outdoor space adjoining a house, used for lounging, dining, etc.

ter·ra cot·ta (ter′ə kot′ə), **1.** *n.* kind of hard, often unglazed, brownish red earthenware, used for vases, statuettes, building decorations, etc. **2.** *adj.* a dull brownish red. *n., pl.* **terra cottas.**

ter·rain (tə rān′), *n.* region of land that is thought of as having particular natural features: *The hilly, rocky terrain of the island made farming difficult.*

ter·rar·i·um (tə rer′ē əm), *n.* a glass enclosure in which plants or small land animals are kept. *n., pl.* **ter·rar·i·ums, ter·rar·i·a** (tə rer′ē ə).

ter·ri·to·ry (ter′ə tôr′ē), *n.* **1.** land belonging to a government; land under the rule of a distant government: *Gibraltar is British territory.* **2.** land; region: *Much territory in northern Africa is desert.* *n., pl.* **ter·ri·to·ries** for 1.

the·oc·ra·cy (thē ok′rə sē), *n.* **1.** government in which God is recognized as the supreme civil ruler and in which religious authorities rule the state as God's representatives. **2.** country or state governed by a theocracy. *n., pl.* **the·oc·ra·cies. –the·o·crat·ic** (thē′ə krat′ik), *adj.*

the·o·rize (thē′ə rīz′), *v.* to form or propose an explanation or explanations based on observation and reasoning: *Scientists have theorized about how life began on Earth.* *v.* **the·o·rized, the·o·riz·ing. –the′o·ri·za′tion,** *n.* **–the′o·riz′er,** *n.*

to·pog·ra·phy (tə pog′rə fē), *n.* **1.** the surface features of a place or region, such as hills, valleys, streams, lakes, bridges, tunnels, roads, etc. **2.** act or process of preparing an accurate and detailed description or drawing of a region's or place's surface features.

trac·tion (trak′shən), *n.* **1.** ability to push against a surface without skidding: *Deep treads improve a car tire's traction in snow or rain.* **2.** a steady pull on an injured bone that helps it heal properly, supplied by a system of weights and pulleys.

trag·ic (traj′ik), *adj.* **1.** of or about a tragedy, or very sad or terrible happening: *a tragic poem.* **2.** very sad; dreadful: *a tragic event.* **–trag′i·cal·ly,** *adv.*

tran·scribe (tran skrīb′), *v.* **1.** to copy in writing or in typewriting: *The minutes of the meeting were transcribed from the secretary's shorthand notes.* **2.** to make a recording, usually on tape, for broadcasting at a later time. *v.* **tran·scribed, tran·scrib·ing. –tran·scrib′er,** *n.*

trans·gress (trans gres′ *or* tranz gres′), *v.* **1.** to break a law, command, etc.; sin. **2.** to go beyond a limit: *Their manners transgress the bounds of good taste.*

trans·gres·sor (trans gres′ər), *n.* person who breaks a law, command, etc.

trans·late (tran slāt′ *or* tranz lāt), *v.* **1.** to change from one language into another: *translate a book from French into English.* **2.** to express one thing in terms of another: *translate words into action.* *v.* **trans·lat·ed, trans·lat·ing. –trans·lat′a·ble,** *adj.*

trans·mis·sion (tran smish′ən *or* tranz mish′ən), *n.* **1.** act or process of sending or passing something from one person, thing, or place to another: *Mosquitoes are the only means of transmission for malaria.* **2.** passage of electromagnetic waves from a transmitter to a receiver: *When transmission is good, even foreign radio stations can be heard.*

trans·mit (tran smit′ *or* tranz mit′), *v.* **1.** to send along; pass along: *I will transmit the money by special messenger. Rats transmit disease.* **2.** to send out signals by means of electromagnetic waves or by wire: *Some station is transmitting every hour of the day.* *v.* **trans·mit·ted, trans·mit·ting. –trans·mit′ta·ble,** *adj.*

trans·par·ent (tran spâr′ ənt), *adj.* **1.** letting light through so that things on the other side can be distinctly seen: *Window glass is transparent.* **2.** easily seen through or detected; obvious: *a transparent excuse.* **–trans·par′ent·ly,** *adv.* **–trans·par′ent·ness,** *n.*

trudge (truj), **1.** *v.* to talk wearily or with effort. **2.** *n.* a hard or weary walk: *a long trudge up the hill.* *v.* **trudged, trudg·ing. –trudg′er,** *n.*

ultraviolet|yield

Uu

ul·tra·vi·o·let (ul′trə vī′ə lit), *adj.* of or about the invisible rays with wavelengths shorter than those of violet light. Ultraviolet rays in sunlight are important to forming Vitamin D, but can cause sunburn.

un·der·grad·u·ate (un′dər graj′ü it), **1.** *n.* student in a college or university who has not yet received a degree. **2.** *adj.* of or for undergraduates.

un·so·cial (un sō′shəl), *adj.* avoiding or lacking a desire to be in the company of others.

us·age (yü′sij), *n.* **1.** the customary way of using words: *The actual usage of speakers and writers of English determines what standard English is.* **2.** way or manner of using or of being used; treatment: *The car has had rough usage.*

Vv

va·lid·i·ty (və lid′ə tē), *n.* **1.** truth or soundness: *the validity of an argument, the validity of an excuse.* **2.** legal soundness or force: *the validity of a contract.*

ven·e·ra·tion (ven′ə rā′shən), *n.* deep respect; reverence.

ven·ti·la·tion (ven′tl ā′shən), *n.* **1.** act or process of supplying with fresh air. **2.** means of supplying fresh air: *Air conditioning provides ventilation in summer.*

ven·ture (ven′chər), **1.** *n.* a risky or daring act, project, or the like: *Our courage was equal to any venture. A lucky venture in oil stock made him rich.* **2.** *v.* to dare to come or go: *We ventured out on the thin ice and fell through.* *v.* **ven·tured, ven·tur·ing.**

ve·rac·i·ty (və ras′ə tē), *n.* **1.** truthfulness. **2.** correctness; accuracy.

ver·dict (vėr′dikt), *n.* **1.** the decision of a jury: *The jury returned a verdict of "Not guilty."* **2.** any decision or judgment: *the verdict of history.*

ver·sa·tile (vėr′sə təl), *adj.* able to do many things well: *She is a versatile student who is skilled at science, art, mathematics, English, German, and history.* **–ver′sa·tile·ly,** *adv.* **–ver′sa·tile·ness, ver′sa·til′i·ty,** *n.* [**Versatile** comes from a Latin word meaning "to turn."]

ver·ti·cal (vėrt′tə kəl), **1.** *adj.* straight up and down; perpendicular to a level surface; upright. **2.** *n.* a vertical line, plane, direction, position, etc. **–ver′ti·cal·ly,** *adv.*

vi·a·duct (vī′ə dukt), *n.* bridge for carrying a road or railroad over a valley, a part of a city, etc.

vo·cal·ist (vō′kə list), *n.* singer.

vo·ca·tion (vō kā′shən), *n.* **1.** occupation, business, profession, or trade: *Architecture is her vocation.* **2.** a strong feeling about, or inclination toward, a certain kind of work, especially religious work.

vo·cif·er·ous (vō sif′ər əs), *adj.* loud and noisy; shouting; clamoring: *a vociferous person, vociferous cheers.* **–vo·cif′er·ous·ly,** *adv.* **–vo·cif′er·ous·ness,** *n.*

vol·a·til·i·ty (vol′ə til′ə tē), *n.* **1.** a tendency toward sudden anger or violence. **2.** tendency to change rapidly from one mood or interest to another; fickleness.

vol·ume (vol′yəm), *n.* **1.** amount of space anything contains or fills: *The storeroom has a volume of 800 cubic feet.* **2.** book forming part of a set or series: *You can find what you want to know in the ninth volume of this encyclopedia.* [**Volume** comes from a Latin word meaning "to roll." Ancient Roman books were rolled scrolls. Big scrolls took up a lot of space, so the space was named for them.]

voy·age (voi′ij), *n.* **1.** a journey by water; cruise: *We had a pleasant voyage to England.* **2.** a journey through the air or through space: *Earth's voyage around the sun.* **–voy′ag·er,** *n.*

Ww

war·rant (wôr′ənt), *n.* **1.** that which gives a right; authority: *He had no warrant to tell us how to behave.* **2.** a written order giving authority for something: *a warrant to search the house.*

Yy

yield (yēld), **1.** *v.* to produce: *This land yields good crops. Mines yield ore.* **2.** *n.* income produced by an investment; profit. **–yield′er,** *n.*

Word Part List

These are the word parts–the roots, prefixes, and suffixes–taught in this book. They are listed in alphabetical order, going from left to right.
Each entry gives you the following information:

- identification of the word part as root, prefix, or suffix
- other ways to spell the word part
- language origin of the word part, usually Latin or Greek
- meaning of the word part
- anchor word that contains the word part to help you remember its meaning

suffix **age**
other spellings ade
origin Latin
meaning action *or* process
anchor word leakage

suffix **ance**
other spellings ence
origin Latin
meaning action, process, *or* state
anchor word annoyance

prefix **anti**
origin Greek
meaning against
anchor word antismoking

root **archy**
other spellings arch
origin Greek
meaning ruler
anchor word monarchy

suffix **ary**
other spellings ory, ery
origin Latin
meaning place for
anchor word library

root **astr**
other spellings aster
origin Greek
meaning star
anchor word astronaut

root **aud**
origin Latin
meaning hear
anchor word audience

root **bene**
origin Latin
meaning good *or* well
anchor word benefit

root **bio**
origin Greek
meaning life
anchor word biology

root **carn**
origin Latin
meaning flesh
anchor word carnivore

root **ceed**
other spellings ced, cess
origin Latin
meaning go
anchor word proceed

prefix **circum**
origin Latin
meaning around
anchor word circumference

root **civ**
origin Latin
meaning citizen
anchor word civilian

root **claim**
other spellings clam
origin Latin
meaning to shout *or* call out
anchor word proclaim

prefix **co**
origin Latin
meaning with *or* together
anchor word copilot

prefix **com**
other spellings con
origin Latin
meaning together *or* with
anchor word companion

root **cosm**
origin Greek
meaning universe *or* world
anchor word cosmos

root **cracy**
other spellings crat
origin Greek
meaning rule
anchor word democracy

root **crit**
origin Greek
meaning judge
anchor word critic

prefix **de**
origin Latin
meaning remove *or* opposite
anchor word deforest

root **dict**
origin Latin
meaning say *or* speak
anchor word predict

root **duct**
other spellings duc
origin Latin
meaning lead
anchor word conductor

prefix **ex**
other spellings e
origin Latin
meaning out
anchor word exit

root **fac**
other spellings fec, fic, fy
origin Latin
meaning make
anchor word factory

root **fer**
origin Greek
meaning bear *or* carry
anchor word fertile

root **geo**
origin Greek
meaning Earth
anchor word geography

root **grad**
origin Latin
meaning step
anchor word grade

root **gram**
origin Greek
meaning thing written
anchor word diagram

root	**graph**
origin	Greek
meaning	to write
anchor word	autograph

root	**gress**
origin	Latin
meaning	go *or* step
anchor word	progress

suffix	**ic**
origin	Latin
meaning	of *or* having to do with
anchor word	comic

prefix	**inter**
origin	Latin
meaning	between
anchor word	interviewer

prefix	**intra**
origin	Latin
meaning	within
anchor word	intrastate

prefix	**intro**
origin	Latin
meaning	in *or* within
anchor word	introduction

suffix	**ist**
origin	Greek
meaning	one who believes, does, or is an expert in something
anchor word	scientist

root	**jud**
origin	Latin
meaning	judge
anchor word	judge

root	**mal**
origin	Latin
meaning	bad
anchor word	malfunction

root	**man**
origin	Latin
meaning	hand
anchor word	manicure

prefix	**mis**
origin	Old English
meaning	badly *or* wrongly
anchor word	mistrustful

root	**mis**
other spellings	mit
origin	Latin
meaning	to send
anchor word	missile

root	**mort**
origin	Latin
meaning	death
anchor word	immortal

root	**nomin**
other spellings	nomen
origin	Latin
meaning	name
anchor word	nominate

prefix	**ob**
other spellings	op
origin	Latin
meaning	toward *or* against
anchor word	object

suffix **ologist**
other spellings logist
origin Greek
meaning a person who studies or is an expert on a subject
anchor word meteorologist

suffix **ology**
other spellings logy
origin Greek
meaning the study of *or* the science of
anchor word meteorology

suffix **ous**
origin Latin
meaning possessing *or* full of
anchor word famous

root **ped**
origin Latin
meaning foot
anchor word pedal

root **phobia**
origin Greek
meaning irrational fear
anchor word phobia

root **phon**
origin Greek
meaning sound
anchor word symphony

root **pod**
origin Greek
meaning foot
anchor word tripod

root **port**
origin Latin
meaning carry
anchor word portable

root **pos**
other spellings pon
origin Latin
meaning put *or* place
anchor word pose

prefix **post**
origin Latin
meaning after
anchor word postscript

prefix **pre**
origin Latin
meaning before
anchor word prepay

prefix **pro**
origin Latin
meaning forward *or* in front of
anchor word propeller

root **pub**
other spellings popul
origin Latin
meaning people
anchor word public

root **ques**
other spellings quir, quer, quis
origin Latin
meaning ask *or* seek
anchor word question

prefix **re**
origin Latin
meaning again
anchor word recapture

prefix **re**
origin Latin
meaning back
anchor word reverse

root **spec**
other spellings spic
origin Latin
meaning look
anchor word spectacle

root **tract**
origin Latin
meaning drag *or* pull
anchor word tractor

root **rect**
origin Latin
meaning straight *or* right
anchor word direction

root **stel**
origin Latin
meaning star
anchor word constellation

prefix **trans**
origin Latin
meaning across, over, *or* through
anchor word transatlantic

prefix **retro**
origin Latin
meaning backward
anchor word retrogress

root **ten**
origin Latin
meaning stretch
anchor word extension cord

root **ven**
other spellings vent
origin Latin
meaning come
anchor word convention

root **scrib**
other spellings script
origin Latin
meaning write
anchor word scribble

root **term**
origin Latin
meaning end
anchor word terminal

root **vent**
origin Latin
meaning wind
anchor word vent

root **soci**
origin Latin
meaning companion
anchor word social

root **terre**
other spellings terra, terri
origin Latin
meaning Earth
anchor word extraterrestrial

root **vert**
other spellings vers
origin Latin
meaning turn
anchor word convert

root	**voc**
origin	Latin
meaning	call
anchor word	vocal

root	**vol**
other spellings	volv
origin	Latin
meaning	roll *or* turn
anchor word	revolution